*Speaking Peace*
*in a Climate of Conflict*

# Speaking Peace
# in a Climate of Conflict

MARILYN MCENTYRE

WILLIAM B. EERDMANS PUBLISHING COMPANY
GRAND RAPIDS, MICHIGAN

Wm. B. Eerdmans Publishing Co.
4035 Park East Court SE, Grand Rapids, Michigan 49546
www.eerdmans.com

26  25  24  23  22  21  20      1  2  3  4  5  6  7

ISBN 978-0-8028-7814-4

**Library of Congress Cataloging-in-Publication Data**

A catalog record for this book is available from
the Library of Congress.

# Contents

# CONTENTS

# Introduction

Words are instruments of survival. We hear a lot of them, from routine exchanges with family over morning coffee to the news on the car radio, from song lyrics we barely register as they play on endless loops in stores to discussions in meetings, phone calls, and, if we're lucky, good conversations with good friends.

As I write this, it's not yet eight in the morning, but I have discussed dreams with my husband, listened to the lectionary readings, heard the morning headlines, and perused a few paragraphs in preparation for the day's work. Already I have taken in more than sufficient words for a day's reflection, but many more are to come. Words, along with images, are writ large on billboards, in shop windows, and on neon signs, filling the urban landscape. On my drive to Berkeley this afternoon I know I will see eye-catching appeals to choose a new healthcare plan, visit a casino, buy vodka or sexy blue jeans or a new smart phone, or repent and receive Jesus's forgiveness. Really. Those of us who inhabit urban and suburban environments have had to adapt to chronic word and image overload. We are assailed from every direction. Those of us who write, teach, or parent, and who play a part in public life, need, more than ever, to equip each other with words that will help us navigate the confusions and challenges of this historical moment.

"Our times," as a lovely passage from *The Book of Common Prayer* puts it, "are in God's hands." Our times are also in ours—the rich, wild internet, the water crisis, widespread warfare, climate change, a polarized economy— these are the conditions in which we are to work out our salvation together, listening to one another, listening for the voice of God in the silence behind all the chatter, and telling stories and singing songs that help, even in the midst of human squalor, to make all things new.

We need to learn new ways to speak peace, reclaiming words that have been weaponized and beating them into plowshares. We need to find words that comfort in the midst of new kinds of distress and sorrow and that sustain courage in the face of large and looming threats. Life-giving conversations require a willingness to wake up, be aware, peer into the darkness, consider and consult and open our imaginations to perilous possibilities. Because it is in that darkness that the Light shines—there where the Word, which was in the beginning, emerges from the deeps of cosmic silence and summons us to listen and learn so that we may hear the word given to each of us to embody and speak into the world while we are here. It is tempting, rather than accept that strenuous invitation, to take refuge in the diverting cacophony, letting idle words wash over us while we float in a river of sound.

Conversation—which once meant "walking with" one another—has historically been the warp and woof of community life. It provides (to switch metaphors) rich soil where thought and feeling can take root and branch and blossom. It equips us to venture out from our circles of trust into the fog of word wars, prepared to speak peace, to practice nonviolent communication, to reclaim and sometimes proclaim words that sound a ring of truth that can be heard above the drone of incessant distractions. These days, it's a little harder to come by—the kind of conversation that does all those things. If we want to make space for it, we have to resist some powerfully erosive forces.

In these pages I offer reflections that have emerged from my own work with words as a reader and writer and teacher, but also from my growing concern about what is happening to words as more and more of them become contaminated and turn into "triggers," as lies go unchallenged and honesty goes unrewarded—or is punished. I have tried to identify a number of strategies for maintaining clarity, integrity, and authenticity in the midst of the morass, drawing examples from contemporary writers and speakers, stewards of words, from whom we can all learn. It is a time to be, as they are, deft and strategic, subversive, surprising, amusing, able to offer the occasional "shock of recognition" that reminds and reawakens. I offer my reflections in gratitude to those who have helped me sustain my own efforts to speak and to live with integrity and hope—to be a better reader, writer, and participant in the long, often contentious conversation we've been called to.

Let's start by considering how good stewards of language equip us to cope with a political discourse that consists largely of hyperbole, *ad hominem* attacks, spin, and sound bites. Increasingly over the past decade, accusations of lies, incompetence, bigotry, and corruption have filled airtime that could have been devoted to much-needed public education on urgent issues, fact-checked, focused, implications made explicit. The airwaves are full of voices shouting at each other from opposite sides of a widening battlefield where arguments over climate change, trade agreements, gay marriage, abortion laws, health care, immigration, and what to do about poverty and homelessness are buried in rhetoric that oversimplifies and obscures what is really at stake. And the battle lines run right down the aisles of churches: congregations split and splinter over how to worship, what the Bible really means, and what faith language to use.

George Orwell famously claimed that one of the reasons writers write at all is to make a political statement, or perhaps to influence political life. It is, in fact, impossible not to write politically: common discourse is charged with political associations that weight the words we use. Common words such as "right" or "duty" or "threat" or "American" or "great"—along with any "ism" you might think of—are difficult to disengage from the partisan contexts in which they're so loudly spoken. Speaking is not a politically or theologically neutral act any more than voting or buying, and the charge words carry is intensified in a climate of widespread verbal promiscuity and word wars.

Richard Mouw, former president of Fuller Seminary, put it this way in his thoughtful book about civility, *Uncommon Decency*:

> One of the real problems in modern life is that the people who are good at being civil often lack strong convictions and people who have strong convictions often lack civility. . . . We need to find a way of combining a civil outlook with a "passionate intensity" about our convictions. The real challenge is to come up with a convicted civility.[1]

To speak or write with "convicted civility" is to speak out in ways that shock, disturb, and indict readers' complacencies without leaving those readers defensive, overwhelmed, or in despair about issues they feel powerless to address. How do we write so as to educate, encourage, and clarify? How do we craft sentences that survive and subvert organized confusion?

I offer the strategies in the coming pages not as an expert, and certainly not as a person who is politically or theologically neutral, but rather as a writer who is still gratefully learning from those who seem to me particularly effective in speaking truth to power, speaking for the poor, speaking up when it's needed, speaking out for those who are silenced, and speaking for the rest of us when they are the ones who are in a position to do so and who recognize the call when it comes.

Sometimes we are the ones who are called. There are moments when we have to recognize that neutrality is complicity and to enter the conversation with clarity, conviction, and a good op-ed piece. It's good, on the one hand, to avoid becoming a self-styled prophet—I'm aware of the temptation to think one has access to a God's-eye view. On the other hand, it's good to be alert to moments when our situation and gifts oblige us to enter public controversies in hope of offering a stay against confusion.

The practices we're going to look at are those of writers who offer and model what we need now. Each of them has helped educate me and has informed my political, theological, and writerly sensibilities. I hope these brief reflections on their ways of seeing and saying may help equip us for opportunities to speak for the common good on social media, in classrooms, in interviews, in op-ed pages, and in city council meetings, university chapel services, service club meetings, conferences, and sermons with clarity, sanity, and grace.

So let us begin by turning our attention to the challenging matter of defining our terms.

## Don't Rely on Webster's

In case you don't get enough email, here's a subscription that will bring a bit of education to your in-box: you can receive a "Word of the Day" direct from Merriam-Webster, a company started by two word lovers that has, since 1828, provided Americans with hefty dictionaries that offer standard spelling, definitions, and updates on the evolution of American English. Even the words I think I know sometimes surprise me. Rather than deleting the word of the day when I "know" it, sometimes I open the page and discover nuances of meaning or odd facts about the word's history. ("Shambles," for instance, once meant "meat market." For more, see Webster's!) The moments it takes to read those little backstories are, I believe, time well spent. "Ordinary" words become a little more mysterious, their meanings shaped and shaded in new ways, and my awareness of their resonance heightened.

One of the newsbreaks I've had to deliver to students over the years is that words' meanings are malleable. When defining terms in papers or speeches, they're not allowed to start any sentence with "According to Webster's" (or even the OED). Rather, "defining key terms" means considering carefully how they have come to understand the word, in what contexts it's used, how those may be specific to this historical moment, to what (and whose) purposes, and what associations they bring to it. "Justice," for instance, has a slightly different range of meaning and associations in the phrase "the justice system," or as a title ("Supreme Court justice"), or as an office ("Department of Justice") than it does as a justification for the American Revolution or as a biblical idea ("To do justice, and to love kindness, and to walk humbly with your God"; Mic. 6:8).

Words, in other words, float in a fluid medium—a river of conversation, written and spoken, that has run a winding course over the centuries, through a wide variety of social landscapes, turning to rapids in times of crisis. To leave that metaphor and think of them in a more mysteriously literal way, words occupy "fields" of meaning; their color and weight are affected by the words around them. Standing alone, they "mean" much less than in sentences, poems, headlines, or homilies.

Meaning is malleable—context-dependent, somewhat dependent on the idiosyncrasies of a particular wordsmith, layered, shaded by irony or obliquity. We need to hold one another accountable for the meanings we make. "What do you mean?" belongs somewhere in every conversation. It's not a simple question, and it rarely calls for a simple answer. It sometimes brings a speaker up short or elicits a defensive parry: "What do you mean, what do I mean? I mean what I say." So we rephrase the question: "What's your understanding of that term?" "Could you give an example of what that might look like in action?" "Are you using that term in the same way your opponent recently used it?"

An even more important question is "What do I mean?" Ask it as you reread your draft, as you peruse the bullet points for your presentation, as you fish for a way to explain "greedy" to a five-year-old—or to a Congressperson considering further tax cuts for large corporations. It's a habit I'd venture to call a spiritual discipline: as I pray for kindness, clarity, and courage in my writing and teaching, it's simply good practice to ask myself, What do I mean by "good" poetry or by "responsible" reading? What does it mean to "develop" a point? What's the difference between making an "appropriate" concession and capitulating? What is "enough"? Who is the "we" in question? When do kids get to see "adult" material? And what do I mean when I stand in a congregation and affirm, "I believe . . ."?

"Believe," by the way, once meant "to hold dear." The Latin word for "believe," *credo*, was derived from an earlier form, *cor do*—"I give my heart." Attention to etymology has its place in spiritual practice: it often serves to remind me of the deeper layers of meaning that enrich the words I use, widen my sense of their consequence, and enliven my sense of what Flannery O'Connor might have called their "sacramentality." Every word has a history. Some of those histories are adventure-laden, war-torn, wild, idiosyncratic; some of them are decorous, fairly linear, and more or less predictable. But even the latter remind us of the longitudinal dimension of language — how words connect us to the "long conversation" and to those who have given them life in prayers, poems, position papers, political documents, encyclicals, laws, and letters.

Disconnecting words from their histories is dangerous. It hollows them out, leaving them gutted like fish—edible, perhaps, but no longer beautiful, sunlit, and alive. Words naturally evolve and change, but that process is quite different from wrenching them out of historical context and whittling them into commercial slogans, or trimming away theological and cultural associations and turning them into behavioral triggers ("Coke gives life," "A diamond is forever," "Like a good neighbor, State Farm is there"). Every time we use a word, we're making—or muddying—word history. It's very hard to unmake the rings of association or suggestion that accumulate when words are co-opted for partisan or commercial use, or to unlink them from spurious images with which they've been paired.

But meanings do morph naturally, in a process not unlike evolutionary adaptation. "Surgery" has come to mean something much more specialized than it used to as surgical techniques have been developed and surgical specialties have diversified. "Person" has assumed a particular clinical meaning for psychologists, and the meaning of the word has been stretched, some would say beyond reasonable definitional limits, to include large corporations whose money is considered a form of "free speech."

Abstract terms need our particular attention. They need to be defined nearly every time we use them, since they're particularly susceptible to manipulation. Ezra Pound's advice to poets, "Go in fear of abstractions," is a good word for all of us. Any conversation about racism, socialism, feminism, elitism, populism, capitalism, or facism needs to begin—and perhaps continue for some time—with reflection on what the term has meant historically and what it has come to mean over the past few news cycles.

Defining terms is, then, a social responsibility and a spiritual discipline. The task devolves in a particular way on scientists and specialists: good popularizers protect us, the general public, from gradual marginalization in conversations that concern us all. We need to know exactly what they (the scientists and specialists)—and we—are talking about when we talk about climate change or nuclear weapons (or nuclear energy) or uranium depletion or long-polymer plastics or soil depletion. Those of us who stopped taking math when it stopped being required might need to be reminded what "elliptical" means when we speak of a poet's elliptical style; or what "exponential" means when we hear it being used simply to indicate rapid, progressive expansion; or that "factor" means a bit more than one more item on the long list of things to consider.

It need not take long, in any composition or conversation, to pause for a defining moment. Sometimes it takes a few words: "'Sexual assault' is used here to include all unpermitted groping or touching." Sometimes it requires a distinction between two common usages: "I use the term 'conservative' not as a party label synonymous with the current Republican platform, but to mean a general disposition to favor traditional values until it's proven we should do otherwise, and to distrust unnecessary government control. We can, of course, argue about what 'unnecessary' might mean." Sometimes it takes longer—a paragraph, a five-minute digression, a prolonged moment of passion when a speaker goes slightly off topic to make sure a key word is lifted up for careful consideration. Frederick Douglass, for instance, in a powerful 1852 Fourth of July speech, devoted a substantial paragraph to reflection on the legal definition of "man" that still excluded enslaved human beings:

> For the present it is enough to affirm the equal manhood of the Negro race. Is it not astonishing that, while we are plowing, planting, and reaping, using all kinds of mechanical tools, erecting houses, constructing bridges, building ships, working in metals of brass, iron, copper, silver, and gold; that while we are reading, writing, and ciphering, acting as clerks, merchants, and secretaries, having among us lawyers, doctors, ministers, poets, authors, editors, orators, and teachers; that we are engaged in all the enterprises common to other men—digging gold in California, capturing the whale in the Pacific, feeding sheep and cattle on the hill-side, living, moving, acting, thinking, planning, living in families as husbands, wives, and children, and above all, confessing and

worshipping the Christian's God, and looking hope-
fully for life and immortality beyond the grave—we
are called upon to prove that we are men?[1]

Personhood continues to be a contested idea and "person"
a contested term that needs to be shielded from the heat
of public rhetoric that might melt and reshape it into an
instrument of deception.

In a similarly profound moment, Elie Wiesel, whose
memories of Auschwitz have helped keep that experience
alive in public consciousness and conscience, paused in
the course of a statement of gratitude for American help
for victims to define a key term by way of warning:

What is indifference? Etymologically, the word
means "no difference." A strange and unnatural state
in which the lines blur between light and darkness,
dusk and dawn, crime and punishment, cruelty and
compassion, good and evil.

What are its courses and inescapable consequences? Is it a philosophy? Is there a philosophy
of indifference conceivable? Can one possibly view
indifference as a virtue? Is it necessary at times to
practice it simply to keep one's sanity, live normally,
enjoy a fine meal and a glass of wine, as the world
around us experiences harrowing upheavals?

Of course, indifference can be tempting—more
than that, seductive. It is so much easier to look away

from victims. It is so much easier to avoid such rude interruptions to our work, our dreams, our hopes. It is, after all, awkward, troublesome, to be involved in another person's pain and despair. Yet, for the person who is indifferent, his or her neighbor are of no consequence. And, therefore, their lives are meaningless. Their hidden or even visible anguish is of no interest. Indifference reduces the other to an abstraction.

Over there, behind the black gates of Auschwitz, the most tragic of all prisoners were the "Muselmänner," as they were called. Wrapped in their torn blankets, they would sit or lie on the ground, staring vacantly into space, unaware of who or where they were, strangers to their surroundings. They no longer felt pain, hunger, thirst. They feared nothing. They felt nothing. They were dead and did not know it.[2]

A word that might seem bland, if not innocuous, is shown here unmasked and menacing—an evil that often masquerades as a regrettable but minor instance of mental sloth. T. S. Eliot rather more mysteriously, but to similar purpose, defined it this way in his final great poem, "Little Gidding":

> There are three conditions which often look
> alike
> Yet differ completely, flourish in the same
> hedgerow:

Attachment to self and to things and to per-
    sons, detachment
From self and from things and from persons;
    and, growing between them, indifference
Which resembles the others as death resem-
    bles life . . .[3]

Beware, both men seem to say, of anyone who reduces indifference to a small and excusable capitulation to ennui or
social fatigue. It is a dire and morbid condition.

It is not only the dark words, though, that need defining and redefining. "Positive" needs to be reclaimed from
those who use it to affirm oversimplified optimism that
forestalls the arduous spiritual work of sustaining hope.
(See, for example, Barbara Ehrenreich's edgy book, *Bright
Sided*, about the dangers of "positive thinking.") "Joy" needs
to be given room to expand beyond the scope of "pleasure."
And "beauty" needs to be reclaimed from the voracious,
predatory control of the "beauty industry." Wendell Berry
accomplishes this kind of reclamation in his unforgettable
description of a beautiful woman, Hannah Coulter:

Her beauty no longer has its source merely in her
physical presence, though that is pleasing enough;
it comes, rather, from some deep equanimity with
which it has accepted the marks of an extraordinary
knowledge of herself, her powers as a person and as
a woman, her mortality.[4]

His definition sets the bar high; it is an idea, and a standard, of beauty to aspire to. To desire it is necessarily to background those marks and measures of beauty that have become so much a part of commercial culture and contributed not a little to the commodification of women and the self-doubt of their daughters.

I want to conclude this reflection on definition with a word of encouragement to my fellow readers, writers, speakers, parents, and participants in public life: we can all do this. All we really have to do is pause long enough to ask ourselves, "What do I mean by that?" or "What does he or she mean?" or, without apology, "What do you mean?" It's a basic, important exercise of freedom to keep those questions alive.

Let's consider five words that deserve to be defined whenever we use them.

**War**

We hear about "war" every day. Though no "war" since World War II has been declared by Congress, the United States has been involved in almost constant international conflicts since then. Over those decades the word "war" has become ubiquitous. Not only has it been appropriated to describe ongoing state-sponsored violence in places to which we send troops; we have grown so used to hearing it used metaphorically that it can sometimes be hard to remember that such uses are metaphoric: war on poverty; war on crime; war on cancer; war on drugs; war on terror; trade wars; culture wars. In "The War Metaphor in Public Policy," theologian James Childress has pointed out the danger of using the word "war" so widely and loosely: "In debating social policy through the language of war, we often forget the moral reality of war."[5] By definition, such wars are open-ended. The word tends to legitimize extra-legal measures, confusion of public and private interests, and considerable license on the part of those who assume the mantle and rhetoric of "warriors" and thereby lay claim to relatively uncritical public support for often hidden, commercial, and partisan agendas. A lot of private money changes hands in support of "wars" whose conduct remains largely unavailable for public scrutiny or ratification.

When we take particular care about how we use the term "war," when we gently insist on reminding ourselves and others what kind of social contract and constitutional constraints bracket an actual declaration of war, and when we call attention to the costs of using the term loosely, we work toward greater accountability. One way to insist on greater care and clarity in the use of the term is to raise questions: Who declared the "war" in question—say, the war on cancer? Who fights it? By whose authority? Who is the enemy? What might happen if we switched metaphors—say, to a race to cure, an exploration of causes, an effort to understand cancer? What if we thought of drugs not as weapons in a war "we" are all fighting, but as one of a number of ways to approach a widespread, complex

CHAPTER 1

problem? What if our description of that problem included acknowledgment that prevention is as important as cure, and that prevention begins, literally, not with swords, but with plowshares: that the causes of cancer include pesticides, chemical fertilizers, air and water pollutants, plastics, and other substances that are produced and marketed at great profit to private companies? Then the term "war" might come to seem a deceptive, or at least inadequate, descriptor for the efforts necessary to grasp and address the problem.

## Peace

The prophet Jeremiah warns against spurious and deceitful declarations of "peace." As the New Living Translation puts it, "They offer superficial treatments for my people's mortal wound. They give assurances of peace when there is no peace" (Jer. 6:14). His words have direct application to current political rhetoric in which "peace," "peacemaking," "peacekeeping," "peaceful solutions," "peace talks," and "peaceful coexistence" cover over a multitude of tensions, conflicts of interest, power plays, incipient threats, and direct contradictions, as in the application of the term "peacekeepers" or "peacekeeping forces" to armed military employed to keep civilian populations under surveillance and control.

One simple, gentle, and persistent act of resistance to the Orwellian Newspeak that declares "War is peace" is the bit of bumper sticker wisdom that urges us to "Wage peace." Quakers, Mennonites, and other groups committed to peacemaking and peacekeeping have devoted several centuries to developing a vigorous, courageous, politically engaged, and spiritually deep understanding of what "peace" might mean and what it takes to "wage" it.

In a nation where well over half our tax dollars are spent on military enterprises, including multibillion-dollar contracts to private weapons manufacturers; where the Pentagon plans to spend a trillion dollars over the next three decades on a new generation of nuclear-armed bombers, submarines, and land- and air-based missiles; and where we already have more than four thousand nuclear warheads in active stockpiles, those who raise a cry for "peace" are up against not only a war of words but a massive edifice that Eisenhower presciently termed the "military-industrial complex." In his 1961 farewell speech as outgoing president, Eisenhower, the five-star general who had led the US troops on D-day, warned, "We must guard against the acquisition of unwarranted influence, whether sought or unsought, by the military-industrial complex. The potential for the disastrous rise of misplaced power exists, and will persist."

Since then we have normalized the "military-industrial complex" as it has become less and less distinguishable from the variegated enterprises of multinational corporations whose concern is less for the common good than for shareholders' wealth. The need to reimagine, and perhaps reinvent, what peace might look like in our time is urgent, and the task requires both a long look into the way war works now and a concerted, committed, thoughtful, prayerful plan for new projects and policies that might help equalize distribution of essential resources; make shelter, food, and health care more accessible for the poor; insure proper care of the ecosystems we all depend on; put reasonable limits on greed; and make room for all points of view to be articulated safely in the public square.

"Peace," it seems to me, would have to include less imprisonment and more mental health care; support for children and the families, teachers, and local communities that seek to nurture and protect them; serious, patient, informed listening across partisan lines to deepen mutual understanding of the concerns that lie behind political posturing; and full, fair, equal access to voting booths and to citizenship for all whose rights the Constitution established. "Peace" has to include safety and diversity and protection without abuse of power. It has to include law enforcement without legalized brutality.

To "speak peace" in the midst of war talk, we need plain words that remind us of original meanings and historical contexts and that will stay with hearers and disturb them into reflection—not simply a list of benevolent abstractions (equality, justice, access, fairness, compassion) but concrete nouns that help us imagine what peace would be like as a shared experience: children eating responsibly grown food, some of it from school gardens; safe and civil conversations in public places where people in circles face one another; well-maintained public parks, trails, forests, and lakes where people can visit and be reconnected with the natural creatures and systems we depend on.

## Health

"Healthy" is an unprotected market label. Foods saturated with sugar and dubious chemical preservatives can be sold in packages sporting the word "healthy" in bright letters. Anyone who has done even a little homework on food production in this country knows something about the dangers of runoff from factory farms where antibiotics and hormones are overused and remain in the runoff from manure-soaked mud fields, infiltrating soil used for food production.

If our food is not healthy, we are not healthy. If we forestall alarm by normalizing obesity, high rates of diabetes, and even cancer, we reduce the incentives to reset our understanding of "health." The World Health Organization defines health as "a state of complete physical, mental and social well-being and not merely the absence of disease or infirmity." I love the word "well-being" in there. It's a deeply subjective term: only I can assess my well-being. The fact that it's not scientifically precise reminds us that health isn't a purely scientific idea. It has indispensable social, spiritual, and even theological dimensions. The 1928 *Book of Common Prayer* includes a rigorous confession that we might do well to revisit periodically. After recognizing how we have "erred and strayed like lost sheep" and "followed too much the devices and desires of our own hearts," it acknowledges that, having "left undone those things which we ought to have done" and "done those things which we ought not to have done," "there is no health in us."

Health, we may infer from that fervent act of awareness, involves staying on a path that serves our deepest purposes—even those we don't fully comprehend; recognizing our need for something beyond our own passing appetites to guide our choices about how to live; aligning action, will, and desire with what we understand as divine will.

That definition sets a high bar. It relates health to peace of mind, peace with neighbor and with God, and a sense of what is (to use another antiquated phrase from the same venerable source) "meet and right." We need to keep our notion of "health" large and hospitable, recognizing how various are cultural eating patterns and other behaviors, how much of what we understand to be "healthy" depends on norms that deserve thoughtful review, and how deep is the theological taproot of that word, related as it is to healing, wholeness, and, through its Latinate lineage, salvation.

## Freedom

We frequently hear "freedom" defined by rights. Abraham Lincoln defined it by hope. "Free labor has the inspiration of hope," he wrote, and added, "pure slavery has no hope."[6]

Franklin Roosevelt proclaimed that all people—not just Americans—should share what he regarded as the four key freedoms: freedom of speech, freedom of worship, freedom from want, and freedom from fear. Each of those invites us to expand our understanding of "rights" to include the common good and to recognize that freedom includes access to goods and services and a social contract that includes care for everyone's safety. Martin Luther King put it this simply: "No one is free until we are all free." Freedom is, by definition, not a matter of independence but of interdependence.

As "freedom" becomes once again a battle cry that legitimates profit-making warfare, surveillance, dispossession, and greed, we need to retrieve the word for better uses. We need to link it to protection of the natural world—the bees that are dying, the soil that is being depleted, the oceans that are filling with plastic and other toxic waste, the species whose habitats are being destroyed. We need to include the whole created order, on which we depend in ways many of us insufficiently understand, in our concern for the freedom of "all."

It takes a lively imagination to connect the dots between the personal freedom we seek and other people's welfare, and to extend our circle of concern to include the nonhuman creatures that give us oxygen, pollinate our plants, fix nitrogen underground, and become our food. Two of the great minds of the twentieth century, Albert Einstein and J. R. R. Tolkien, converge in linking freedom to imagination.

Tolkien, defending fiction as an exercise of the free imagination, winsomely said, "If a soldier is imprisoned by the enemy, don't we consider it his duty to escape? . . . If we value the freedom of mind and soul, if we're partisans of liberty, then it's our plain duty to escape, and to take as many people with us as we can!"[7] The *Lord of the Rings* trilogy offers all of us a journey through darkness, guided by light shining in unexpected places, where help comes, gracious and timely, and the humble are exalted. It's good to go there, or to Narnia, or to Olympus, or to the ocean where a white whale still lurks. Stories encourage in us the habits of mind and heart that keep us free. Einstein, coming from a very different corner of the creative world, claimed, "Imagination is more important than knowledge. Knowledge is limited. Imagination encircles the world." Imagination, I would add, as many have recognized, is the beginning of compassion, and compassion is where truth becomes a lived experience rather than an abstract proposition.

"You will know the truth," Jesus assured the disciples, "if you continue in my word," and he added the expansive promise that "the truth will make you free" (John 8:31–32). Freedom of this kind is relational, spiritual, mysterious, patient, and incompatible with lies. It is dependent on the humility that is the ground of our humanness—knowing we are not God.

"Humility," Eliot strangely and memorably wrote in his *Four Quartets*, "is endless." Freedom rooted in that soil makes us free indeed.

## Love

Overused, sentimentalized, trivialized, confused with its facsimiles, "love" needs rehabilitation. It seems ironic that English, a language more than usually rich in synonyms and circumlocutions, has to make this little word stretch to serve so many purposes, some of them at odds. The Greeks, with their four words for love (*storgē, philia, erōs, agapē*)—and they had more to use for the applications rippling outward from the concept—offered ready ways to make suitable distinctions among the kinds of love that bind us, teach us, enlarge us, and call us out of ourselves and into marvelous light. Empathy, friendship, romantic love, and unconditional "God love" involve different spiritual practices, disciplines, and levels of spiritual development and self-knowledge.

Paul's rich description of love in 1 Corinthians 13 is read at many weddings, and it provides as fine, multifaceted a definition of the word as any ever written:

> Love is patient; love is kind; love is not envious or boastful or arrogant or rude. It does not insist on its own way; it is not irritable or resentful; it does not rejoice in wrongdoing, but rejoices in the truth. It bears all things, believes all things, hopes all things, endures all things. Love never ends. (1 Cor. 13:4–8)

Each of these qualities is both a function and a feature of love, and each deserves to be unfolded and explored in its own right. We see love here as right action and attitude. We see it linked to joy and generosity and persistence. If we want to keep the word sharpened for precise use, we might regularly direct ourselves and others to this passage.

Raymond Carver's title "What We Talk about When We Talk about Love" offers a simple, even amusing, reminder that we have to have the meta-conversation about love when we use the word, pausing to define, explain, or elaborate what, exactly, we are talking about. It's good for us to search for and use the synonyms we have, to enable one another to make important distinctions as we open our hearts and form our expectations: "affection," "camaraderie," "benevolence," "compassion," "delight," "attentiveness." Real love is nothing if not specific. The words we bring to it are best when they lead us to see one another, and all that is, wholeheartedly, in a new light.

2

## *Unmask Euphemisms*

"Collateral damage" is an insidious and consequential euphemism. It generally refers to the "unintentional" harm done to civilians, property, animals, farmland, schools, and hospitals that lie between bombs or drones and their targets. Wikipedia, where definitions reflect some degree of consensus, describes it as "the incidental killing or wounding of non-combatants or damage to non-combatant property during an attack on a legitimate military target." The term allows those who use it to reduce those horrors—the grieving parents, the scattered bits of wedding feasts, the curled fists of outraged elders, the broken pots and bloodstained rugs, the terrified eyes of children, the long-term deprivations—to abstractions. "Collateral damage" is a sanitary term that sews all that up to be tucked away just outside the closed circle of conscience.

Euphemisms, at their best, are instruments of diplomacy. At their worst they are trapdoors that provide escape routes from responsibility and provide protection for hidden agendas. They are often abstractions (like "economic growth," for instance)—insidious in their own right—that dull the edges of those painful particulars that stab the conscience or awaken concern. Many of them take deep root in popular speech and become so familiar we forget they are masks, but even those that seem innocuous do harm to the extent that they veil truth and forestall a full reckoning with complex facts. George Orwell put it bluntly in his widely read essay "Politics and the English Language." Speaking of euphemistic language in political discourse, he pointed out that its main purpose is "to make lies sound truthful and murder respectable."[1] If that description sounds familiar, it's because it is.

In *The Beauty Myth*, Naomi Wolf takes on euphemistic terms that persuade women to risk their health and well-being on false pretenses: "Cosmetic surgery is not 'cosmetic,'" she writes,

> and human flesh is not "plastic." Even the names trivialize what it is. It's not like ironing wrinkles in fabric, or tuning up a car, or altering outmoded clothes, the current metaphors. Trivialization and infantilization pervade the surgeons' language when they speak to women: "a nip," a "tummy tuck." . . . Surgery changes one forever, the mind as well as the body.[2]

Even more consequential than euphemisms that divert and distract us into pursuit of specious happiness are those that lead us to accept cruelty. Stephen Miles, MD, introduces his courageous book *Oath Betrayed: Torture, Medical Complicity, and the War on Terror* by explaining his decisions about how to speak of torture to people who don't really want to hear about it. Rejecting common newspaper rhetoric, he writes,

> I have avoided euphemisms. For example, I refer to the inmates of the US facilities at Guantanamo Bay, in Iraq, and in Afghanistan as "prisoners" rather than "detainees," "persons under control" (militarily abbreviated "PUCs" and pronounced "pucks"), or "illegal combatants," terms that the government created for the purpose of exempting itself from international norms of civilized conduct.[3]

The common substitution of "gloves off" "interrogation procedures"—or the technical term, "extraordinary rendition"—for "torture" allows us to maintain a comfortable academic distance from the extreme sufferings we sanction when we refuse to speak of them.

That refusal can also take the benevolent form of "positive thinking"—a term that, itself, sometimes serves as a euphemism for moral abdication. In her recent book *Bright-Sided*, Barbara Ehrenreich argues that positive thinking is dangerous because it diverts us from the difficult but necessary task of taking full and adequate account of risks and warning signs in order to devise adequate solutions to looming problems. Those solutions require not only a willingness to know but also honest and informed debate.

Unmasking euphemisms can be accomplished with more or less humor, more or less compassion for those who find comfort in them and respite from the overwhelming problems that can threaten peace of mind and drive us into depression. Those who unmask them perform the work of what I call ordinary prophets, which is to remind people of what they already know but are all too willing to forget. Sometimes this can take the form of a simple request: "Could you say a little more about what you mean by 'acceptable risk'?" Sometimes it can take the form of a question that challenges the assumptions upon which a convenient euphemistic phrase rests: "How is 'national security' separable from the global common good?" Sometimes statistics help: "When you talk about strikes on 'military targets,' how do you think about the 250,000 civilian deaths in Iraq, Pakistan, and Afghanistan in the course of the recent and ongoing wars there?" Sometimes one can make a demand for more careful distinctions: "How would you distinguish the 'alt-right' from neo-Nazis or white supremacists?" These kinds of questions help hold others—and ourselves—accountable when we have the courage to ask them and the wisdom to ask them openheartedly (though not without the urgency of moral concern), willing to listen carefully to the answers. Though some answers are likely to be defensive or even hostile, it's surprising how many people are willing to consider uncomfortable questions they may not recently have asked themselves.

Though it seems safe to assume that many of us accept and use even dangerous euphemisms somewhat passively or without sufficient critical scrutiny, it is equally safe to assume that many of those turns of phrase are deliberate devices—not at all accidental—to deceive the public for power and profit. Our susceptibility to deception is neither innocent nor innocuous; as citizens, consumers, members of families and faith communities, we have an ongoing responsibility to be as "sober" and "watchful" (1 Pet. 5:8 RSV) with respect to language practices as we are with respect to public policies and personal habits. We need to ask ourselves in all those areas, (1) Does this practice or policy do harm? If so, to whom, and how can that harm be mitigated? (2) Whose interests does this practice or policy most directly serve? Are those who stand to profit from it open about their interests? Are those interests in conflict with the common good? (3) How have we/I normalized this practice? How do I tend to hide even from myself the hidden costs and consequences of this practice? Applying these questions to our word choices, as to our voting choices or food choices, can yield surprising results: we may come uncomfortably to recognize what we have been supporting by agreeing to renamings that weaken the impact of important truths.

To challenge euphemisms is not necessarily to suggest that they don't sometimes serve a legitimate purpose, or that candor is always free of bias, or that literal terms are preferable to polite language. But because euphemisms so often obscure hard and necessary truths, we need to be vigilant about keeping those truths visible.

Traditional cultures recognize the power of names and naming in stories and in rituals such as the vision quest, which often involves finding or receiving a new name. Elders confer meaningful names on people and places by way of blessing and direction. Christening and baptismal rites still focus attention not only on bringing a child into the embrace of the community of faith but also on giving that child a name—an act that canon and civil law recognize as binding and authoritative. These legacies, vestigial as they sometimes seem, remind us that names have weight, that they connect us and sometimes inculpate us, give us access to and a claim upon those whose names we share or who have called us by name. They also remind us that the power to confer and inscribe a name is not to be treated lightly. The bishop dons his or her miter, the tribal elder his or her ceremonial headdress, and in other traditions ceremonial garb or objects are brought to set the act apart from others.

When products are named, or policies or military campaigns are given code names, those involved are similarly convinced of the importance of the names they confer, but often those calculations are private and privileged; they take place in boardrooms and strategy sessions where marketers or investors or pollsters or politicians meet to consider who is likely to "buy in" to their representation of the product or plan, and how a careful redescription might forestall critical questions. Think, for example, of these loaded names for military actions: "shock and awe," "Operation Enduring Freedom," "Operation Valiant Guardian." Or think of what we euphemistically call "reform" bills or "development projects" or "memory care" facilities or "neighborhood clean-up campaigns."

Cultures differ, of course, in what they veil with euphemisms, depending on attitudes toward the body, sex, illness, disability, and death, as well as class, money, and war. It is safe to say that behind every euphemism lies a secret—a practice or fact that cannot bear direct public scrutiny. Some are relatively harmless nods to class-bound notions of propriety: calling a lavatory a "restroom," for instance, or genitals "private parts." Some are deliberate efforts to accord greater respect to people who have been demeaned or excluded by labeling: "cripples" gave way to "the disabled," which in turn became "people with disabilities," in an effort to separate personhood from physical or mental limitations, and "differently abled," in an effort to recognize the ways adaptation can develop important skills and gifts.

But euphemistic language appears and spreads most abundantly where acts that are morally offensive—sometimes crimes against humanity—are made to seem right and necessary by those they are likely to benefit: exploitation of labor, moving young girls from poverty into prostitution, dropping bombs in the vicinity of schools or hospitals, or violently expropriating homes and lands for purposes of "expansion" or "improvement" or, more gloriously, "manifest destiny." It is instructive to take stock of what actions and policies our culture most commonly "euphemizes" and to consider the moral consequences of the lies and half-truths we have come to accept, if only by incessant reiteration. A short inventory of those areas of life we consistently soften or spin by means of euphemisms might provide a kind of *examen* (examination of conscience) for those of us who either unwittingly or unwillingly participate in domesticating deception. Medicine, law, education, fashion, and the food and fuel industries have their own lexicons of language that sidesteps hard truths or reinforces social power (say, with pretentious titles) or dresses up drudgery or obscure hazards. Some lead us to accept costly policy decisions without much objection: cuts become "savings," for example. Killing a living fetus, often violently, is neutralized as "termination of pregnancy."

An article in *The Economist* cited a number of common euphemisms used in the buying and selling of real estate as a wry example of the ways marketing depends upon slight (or not so slight) deceptions:

> A "bijou" residence is tiny (it may also be "charming", "cosy" or "compact"). A "vibrant" neighbourhood is deafeningly noisy; if it is "up and coming" it is terrifyingly crime-ridden, whereas a "stone's throw from"

means in reach of a powerful catapult. Conversely, "convenient for" means "unpleasantly close to". "Characterful" means the previous owner was mad or squalid. "Scope for renovation" means decrepit; "would suit an enthusiast" means a ruin fit only for a madman.[4]

Though the writer exaggerates to make a point, the point is that euphemisms distort, in this case like flattering mirrors, to bypass our three most useful defenses: rational thought, gut feelings, and core values. Decision-making is less reliable or efficient when it involves second-guessing, decoding, and well-tempered temptation.

In their article "Euphemisms and Ethics," Jeremy Fyke and Kristin Lucas looked at language use by those who reported, covered up, and investigated the long-term sex scandal that was disclosed at Penn State in 2001 and received considerable media attention in the long aftermath. Those who reported the egregious behaviors, they pointed out, used coded language to report the assaults to administrators, freeing those administrators to deceive themselves and the public by means of deliberate distortions that the euphemisms invited and allowed. In one instance, sexual assault was referred to as "horsing around."[5] Euphemistic language, they conclude, "impairs decision-making" and forestalls healthy criticism within institutions. All institutions have some; euphemisms grow like crabgrass in the chemically fertilized soil of institutional life and reflect the concerns and assumptions of the people in power.

Naming is an exercise of power. Renaming involves a transfer of power. Unnaming is a stripping of power from those unnamed, and often an abuse of power on the part of those who presume to reduce names to numbers, for instance. It takes courage to name what is being deliberately and defensively obscured. Plain language is not always welcome. Quakers' historical commitment to plain speaking—avoiding class-based titles, avoiding hyperbole, flattery, jargon, and indirection—is worth mentioning here for the way it links faith practice to accuracy and clarity and the way it reminds us that words are acts and acts have consequences.

Let's consider, for example, the consequences of six dangerous euphemisms and what it might mean to resist the seductions they offer.

## Detention

We've heard a great deal in recent months about detainees, detention centers, and children and families being held in "detention" while awaiting either asylum or deportation. In her article "Smoke Screens: Is There a Correlation between Migration Euphemisms and the Language of Detention?," Mariette Grange suggests, "While language used to describe migrants and asylum-seekers is often euphemistic (or dysphemistic), tending to dehumanize them, language used to characterize their treatment in custody appears aimed at shielding detention from scrutiny." She argues, as others have, that the effects of misleading language on policy and public perceptions in the area of immigration rights are significant.[6]

The difference between "detention" and "imprisonment" seems fairly obvious: most of us would object to "imprisoning" children, but some might be a little more open to "detaining" them. Detaining someone suggests at most a temporary delay: "I'm sorry I'm late—I was detained by a conference call at the office." "The kids who participated in the cafeteria food fight were detained after school." But the term has been stretched to describe stays that in 2018 (according to the *Houston Chronicle*) averaged seventy-five days for immigrant children held in separate facilities from parents;[7] stays for "terrorism suspects" while they await due process sometimes extend to years.

The relatively benign term "detention center" tends to forestall public outrage or serious investigation of the conditions in most of those facilities. A report by the US Civil Rights Commission reminds readers that, "in theory, detention is temporary and for administrative purposes only." However, it goes on, "in reality, apprehended children are often detained for longer periods of time than necessary. They are separated from their families and exposed to conditions that don't meet the government's child-protection standards." Meanwhile, adults are "held in conditions similar to criminal incarceration in violation of standards of civil detention."[8]

Without due process or constitutional protections,

many, including some children, are brought there in shackles; most belongings will be confiscated; little privacy is afforded; abuses, including sexual assault and refusal of medical care, are common.

Using the term "imprisonment" would move us in the direction of accountability and encourage more vigorous action on behalf of those being held without bail and without any criminal charges. The fact that detention has, in fact, become a widespread form of extralegal imprisonment is a matter people of conscience need to reckon with.

### Electronic Persons

The European Parliament is considering assigning the legal status of "electronic person" to autonomous robots. Robots could be held responsible for their actions and could enter into legal agreements. The analogy with making corporations "persons" under law is close: legal responsibility is not the same as moral responsibility, but giving robots the former could tend to absolve those who own or program them of the latter. Still, they are designed to serve the purposes of the real people who own them. Their personhood, one writer points out, "is then also a fiction that merely exists to facilitate [this benefit]. . . . The robot does not suddenly gain rights and obligations similar to those of humans, but rather the owner behind the robot sets up a legal fiction, of which he is in control, much like a (majority) shareholder." Moreover, the writer continues, "if a clear division were to be made between owner and robot, this would also mean a limited liability for the owner in case of situations that are not covered under insurance. The electronic person would only be required to pay insofar as it is solvent. In practice, this means that the owner of a robot is only liable for the robot to the extent of the capital that the owner has invested in the electronic person."[9]

It doesn't take a law degree to recognize dangers in the notion of electronic "personhood." It is not hard to see upon very little reflection that, rather than inviting particular respect for the technological achievement robots represent—a very human achievement—it tends rather to reduce "personhood" to a legal convenience, stripping it of its historical and metaphysical importance. What we have come to call "human rights"—the right of all "persons" to life, liberty, and the pursuit of happiness, the assurance that no "person" shall be held for a capital crime without a jury indictment, the right of all "persons" to equal protection under the law—might be at risk if they were extended to "electronic persons."

To introduce an odd analogy, I once heard a ranger in a national park speak about the danger of personification of wildlife in the park's wild spaces. Bears have so often, in stories and on videos made for children, been benevolently personified that the real dangers they represent become obscured, and tragic maulings have occurred because of such conditioned miscalculation of the risks. Similarly, personifying machines of our own making would tend to obscure the kind of power they represent, the ways in which they might tend to displace or misdirect human sympathies and identification, and the question of our right relationship to the manufactured world. "Robot" keeps the distinction clear.

## Settlements

"Settlement" is a neutral-sounding term. When it is used to describe the relocation of Jewish Israelis to places long occupied by Arab Palestinian people, however, it masks a great deal of violence—destruction of homes, expropriation of ancestral lands, and displacement and deprivation of families. It helps obscure these realities by suggesting that occupation of Palestinian territory is a matter of more or less natural demographic shift, not unlike building new housing developments anywhere. (Though gentrification—"settlements" of the affluent who rebuild in areas where the poor have found affordable housing, without proper provision for displaced occupants—might be seen as a smaller-scale analogue to occupation.) In 2006 the BBC published a list of key terms used in the ongoing Israeli-Palestinian conflict, defining "settlement" in this way: "Settlements are residential areas built by Israelis in the occupied territories. They are illegal under international law: this is the position of the UN Security Council and the UK government among others—although Israel rejects this."[10] The term serves to confuse the general public both inside and outside Israel about the processes and human costs of relocation and paralyzes effective pursuit of resolution and peace in the region.

## Harvesting

Originally this word referred to the work of reaping and gathering crops cultivated for human use. It is now also used, however, to refer to (1) killing or taking wild animals and plants from their native habitat for personal use, or (2) taking organs from a recently deceased donor, or (3) gathering data from large systems like Google or Facebook, through which billions of data bytes pass every day. Each of these latter uses is problematic; in each case "harvesting" is a euphemism that invites a false analogy. Let's take them one by one.

"Harvesting" wild animals blurs the distinction between what we have a right to by cultivation, investment of personal labor and resources, and participation in a food system that, however imperfect, is subject to some regulation. The term also masks the simple fact that such work involves killing, often endangering species and habitats. Part of maintaining adequate oversight of consequential processes by which we get and use what we need from the earth is acknowledging with care how we understand ownership, property rights, access rights, and ecological consequences.

"Harvesting" organs is a similarly curious and arguably offensive way of speaking about removing organs from a recently deceased person for immediate transplant into a living patient's body. Though some donation organizations have ceased to use this term, others continue to speak of "harvesting" organs, though the usage suggests weirdly that those organs were being grown for this purpose; it implies an instrumental view of the human body, reducing it, in effect, to a site of production. The preferable term, now prescribed by organizations such as Donate Life, is "recovering" organs.

Corporations that "harvest" data also "mine" or "extract" or "scrape" it; the terms are often used interchangeably. All of them liken the process of gathering data from users to taking something from the earth for human use. "Harvesting," in particular, indicates the time-sensitive nature of such an endeavor: some data, as on Twitter, disappear after a specified period and so must be gathered while "fresh." The verb obscures the fact that much of that data is taken without users' knowledge, that users don't know (and sometimes the "harvesters" don't yet know) to what uses that information will be put, and that the business of data gathering still takes place in a legal gray area. By way of example, consider the fact that because of the data they "harvest," Google knows where I've been since I began using my phone, which events I've attended, the sites I've searched, what kinds of products I shop for, what I watch on YouTube, and what apps I use. Facebook has every message and file I've sent on their site, all my phone contact data, and the audio messages I've received or sent. We should at the very least be watchful for breaches of privacy and erosion of basic protections. For a fascinating, in-depth analysis of the process and implications of the commodification and trading of human behavioral data, see Shoshana Zuboff's *The Age of Surveillance Capitalism.*[11]

## Humanitarian Intervention

More than a century ago, the British statesman Sir William V. Harcourt, writing under the pen name Historicus, defined "intervention" as "a high and summary procedure that can sometimes snatch a remedy beyond the reach of law. As in the case of revolution, its essence is its illegality and its justification is its success."[12] He might also have made the comparison with invasion; intervention is often, if not a direct act of war, at least an arrogation of authority to intervene in affairs of another sovereign state. Richard Falk helpfully clarifies three dimensions of "humanitarian intervention" that often entangle justifications in confusing ways. (1) The political dimension of the term, he points out, has to do with the effectiveness and acceptability of an intervention as it serves the interests of the intervening state. (2) The moral dimension has to do with how it "benefits the peoples of the target society, serves the values (and interests) of the intervening state, and contributes to the global common good." (3) The legal dimension has to do with "invoking and establishing precedents and making legal arguments about rules and standards in support of, or in opposition to, a particular interventionary undertaking."[13]

So-called humanitarian interventions are often conducted by armed forces and serve unacknowledged purposes. No intervention is apolitical. No consensus has been reached among nations about the legitimacy of humanitarian intervention and the conditions under which it could be legitimized.

One reason the term is problematic is that it is not altogether oxymoronic: intervention to prevent large-scale abuses, wanton violence toward civilians, and genocide would seem to be a moral imperative. Yet the term opens a Pandora's box of possibilities for abuse, since it is such a ready tool for legitimizing military action that serves private agendas.

## Development/Developers

The World Bank has eliminated the term "developing" as a descriptor for the 159 countries to which the UN has applied that label because, as reporter Tim Fernholz points out, "nobody has ever agreed on a definition for these terms in the first place."[14] Many use the term even if the country or region described is not actually developing. But the problem goes further than that. In the fields of development economics and development policy, the term is generally connected to certain measurements of individual and municipal or national well-being—to thriving. But of course those are still abstractions, and they often beg the question of who is thriving at whose expense.

"Development" often refers to acquiring infrastructures such as roads and bridges, wells and electronic networking, that enable ongoing communication, economic exchange, and consumer education. Without going into the extensive theory on development of complex adaptive systems, my purpose here is simply to note that the term can become a euphemism that masks forfeitures involved in development—often certain stabilizing and nurturing dimensions of local community life, local businesses, social and intergenerational integration, and authentic relationships between producers and consumers of goods and services. At the same time, it elides the question of who stands to benefit. Real estate development in California, my home state, for instance, is generally still advertised to the public as a benefit to the community, though the state's limited water resources have been a matter of fierce contention for years, as urban and agricultural access is stretched in periods of extended drought.

A simple question that needs to be raised when one hears about "developing" countries or promising new "developments" in science or industry or housing is, What is being developed, and for whom? As with every abstraction, we need to tie the word to actualities to keep it from floating into the euphemistic ether where it can do as much harm as carbon.

3

*Remind People of What They Know*

It's surprising how effective and important the humble task of reminding can be. It is required daily of teachers, preachers, and parents. Forgetting is an ancient human tendency; it was certainly one of the besetting sins of a people who throughout the Old Testament had to be reminded—sometimes sharply and painfully—of God's mercy, justice, faithfulness, guidance, and glory. They also had to be reminded not to worship golden calves or cheat or lie. I once asked a colleague what she would tell her undergraduates if she had one sermon to leave them with. "That's easy," she replied. "Don't lie." It's pretty basic. It's something we all know. We need to be reminded.

Especially over the years since 9/11, as threats of "terrorism" have been used to justify chronic warfare, we have needed reminders about who we are (or have hoped to be) as a people whose citizenship and public commitments are complicated by remote-controlled wars, drones, xenophobia, and the polarization of poverty and privilege. In *The End of America: Letter of Warning to a Young Patriot*, Naomi Wolf, recognizing our need for prophetic reiteration, writes this reminder of what we all learned about the Declaration of Independence and the Constitution in high school civics:

> Those words at the time they were written were blazingly, electrifyingly subversive. If you understand them truly now, they still are. You are not taught—and it is a disgrace that you aren't—that these men and women were radicals for liberty; that they had a vision of equality that was a slap in the face of what the rest of their world understood to be the unchanging, God-given order of nations; and that they were willing to die to make that desperate vision into a reality for people like us, whom they would never live to see.[1]

The slap in the face is not an idle metaphor; the book offers its own version of a sharp wake-up call, as well as a redefinition of patriotism and a strong rejection of the triumphalist rhetoric that has abounded since 9/11 and the "Patriot Act" that followed in its aftermath, which let loose a string of lasting consequences.

Citing Jefferson, Franklin, and their fellow revolutionaries, Wolf summons us back to the wisdom of founding documents, flawed as their authors may have been by sexual and economic privilege and, tragically, by slaveholding. Their intelligent guidance about peaceful transition, checks on personal power, and balances among policy-making bodies needs to be kept available, along with the Bible, Shakespeare, St. Augustine, Lao-Tse, Gandhi, St. Teresa, Dostoevsky, and Desmond Tutu, just to pull a few names from the vast communion of saints and scribes we rely on. Returning to known, seasoned sources of wisdom reminds us that our own judgments have their roots in time past, and in the long conversation we call culture.

Those of us who teach, preach, parent, serve on boards, or occupy administrative positions in institutions are all called to be reminders (or, as I like to put it, re-minders, since the hyphen calls attention to the condition of mindfulness to which we hope to return). For leaders in institutions and organizations, being a reminder means having read the faculty handbook or by-laws carefully enough to cite them when conflicts arise that earlier generations foresaw. It may mean being the person who actually knows *Robert's Rules of Order* and can wield that tool to help navigate difficult conversations. For preachers it means returning to familiar texts with open hearts and a "beginner's mind," making them relevant and accessible for those who might otherwise relegate them to antiquity. For journalists, artists, and musicians, reminding means plumbing the past for techniques, ideas, themes, and interesting problems in order to turn those to present purposes. For parents it means patient, loving repetition: teaching gratitude by prompting the "Thank-you," teaching responsibility by reciting the familiar list of chores, withstanding rolled eyes and occasional whining for the sake of fostering life-giving habits of mind and heart. Reminding means revisiting, repeating, reframing, restoring, renewing. Reminders are keepers of the long stories—history, sacred texts, sacred objects, human memory—that provide backdrop, source, and vocabulary for our personal stories.

I remember vividly the moment when, in high school, listening to a beloved history teacher describe class warfare, I became aware of where my own life might be situated on a socioeconomic scale. I learned to locate myself in terms of race, class, gender, religion, age, sexual orientation, and consumer preferences. Once awareness of that web of social identities takes root in our consciousness, it can be hard to find our way back to the deep center where the Self is a mystery—the Self we might call soul—the Self that encounters God. We need those who remind us of who we are called to be, mirroring what we cannot see for ourselves and, importantly, finding language that isn't confined to psychological, sociological, or political categories, but lifts us into a different kind of awareness, subtler, older, more mysterious.

We need language that reminds us of who we are so that we don't fall into a facile and dangerous habit of identifying ourselves simply as consumers, or feminists, or Republicans or Democrats, or even as citizens, or members of a particular family or tribe, important as those may be. The "I" who lives in the deepest places of psyche and soul, known fully only to God, is unique. That Self cannot be objectified or commodified or regulated into unthinking obedience to tyrants. We need prophets—and I use the term advisedly—who remind us of the mystery that precedes even the commingling of DNA strands in the conjoined sperm and egg. The prophetic word summons us to awareness not only of what is unfolding before us, reading signs of what is to come, but also of what lies behind us, beneath us, within us, and beyond us in that realm where, as Paul put it, our lives are "hidden with Christ in God" (Col. 3:3).

Every time I witness a baptism I am moved by the words, "See what love God has for us, that we should be called children of God, for so we are." I need that reminder. None of my human roles takes precedence over that redeeming fact: that I am a child of God; that I have been called by name. Baptism is only one of the many liturgical ceremonies of reminding that strengthen and renew awareness of and commitment to what we are about. All liturgy is a reminding.

We say the creed again. We hear the Eucharistic prayers again. We sing the hymns again. One I grew up with is a veritable celebration of repetition: "I love to tell the story, for those who know it best seem hungering and thirsting to hear it like the rest."[2] Every week I need the rites of confession and forgiveness. I need to be reminded of the fact of forgiveness. I need to be reminded of what we're doing together in worship: "We praise you, we bless you, we worship you, we glorify you, we give you thanks. . . ." We may be a little tired or restless or even (alas) bored, but the words recall us to the reason we have come. Speaking them, we enter into truths we may not feel at the moment, but need to remember.

My father, raised in a generation and a brand of evangelicalism that harbored strong suspicions of anything "papist," criticized Roman Catholics for their ritual practices by citing (usually in King James English) Jesus's warnings about "vain repetition": "But when ye pray, use not vain repetitions, as the heathen do: for they think that they shall be heard for their much speaking" (Matt. 6:7). It took me a long time to recognize the fact that not all repetition is vain. We live by repetition—of heartbeat and breath, of words like "I love you," of maxims that become grounding points, of lines or phrases remembered and cherished for the life-giving energy they rekindle. Still, the warning about vain repetition is an interesting one. It invites us to ponder the difference between vain or tedious or anxious repetition and the reminding that keeps our hearts open and our attention focused on what matters.

Repetition of the latter kind—reminding—is a skill and an art form. The best reminders tell us what we already know in ways that make it new every morning. They do this by various means. One of the most essential is attention to words themselves, lifting up words that have weight and resonance, history or shock value, largeness or etymological depth. Take, for example, the word "remember" that occurs in so many rites. It should, occasionally, give us pause: What do we actually do when we remember? It's the opposite of "dismember": we bring back together what has been broken apart, or what has diffused or dispersed or dissolved. We reassemble the pieces of a story, not like puzzle pieces that can fit together in only one way, but like elements in a collage, seeing once again how they might be related, allowing ourselves to foreground some parts of the story and background others, as need and the pressures of the historical moment seem to require. Remembering is a complex, creative act, not at all simple, though it can erode into sentimentality or nostalgia for the past. Good reminders teach us how to remember.

Remembering is not only a reenvisioning of the past, but a way of understanding the present. When we encounter what is new, we scan it for whatever connects it to what we already know. We make analogies and comparisons. We recognize whatever is familiar in it. But recognition, like remembering, is not a simple matter. A moment of recognition—seeing traces of the known in the unknown—can rekindle the surprise of original encounter as we *re-cognize* (think again) about what we're seeing. I think of those moments when, as a parent, I began an important moment of reminding with "Look at me." Full eye contact, full attention, a full stop to current distractions at least made it possible for my children to hear again what they thought they knew—that it was important to clean up after themselves, or apologize, or share. I wanted them to hear those instructions in a new, more nuanced way, as they matured. I wanted them to internalize not only the instruction, but the reasons for it, the ways in which it called them into a shared life we all had to foster kindly, the ways in which it related to love. We needed to have new conversations laced with the traces of older, more familiar ones.

All the imperatives that have to do with reminding are worth parsing now and then. We need to polish these words like silver to keep them from tarnishing: "remember," "recall," "pay attention," "notice," "look again," "reconsider," "keep," "hold," "ponder," "cherish." If, as reminders, we can invite those whose lives are linked to ours into life-giving listening and speaking practices, beginning with a sharpened awareness of what words carry, our knowing will be alive and resilient and dynamic, open to being reshaped and reformed. There are those among us whose work as reminders offers us models of this undersung but important task. Let me offer three examples of "reminders"—people whose work has been to remind readers and listeners of what we need to know, to keep knowing, and to keep knowing in new contexts for the common good and for the sake of authentic understanding.

## Wendell Berry

When I mention Berry's name, it is often greeted with a knowing, enthusiastic nod. Fans find and recognize each other. Many of us have found lifelines in his novels or poems or essays. They call us to cherish the natural world, make peace with our neighbors, live modestly, care for what we own, question the very fact of ownership, challenge abuses of power, take the long view of life and history. He does not deliver new news. He delivers old news that is newly urgent. In one of his most popular poems, "Manifesto: The Mad Farmer Liberation Front," he delivers reminders in a series of short imperatives, some of them wry, some sobering. These opening lines, for instance, mirror for readers the unhealthy norms many of us have become accustomed to in urbanized, secular, capitalistic culture:

> Love the quick profit, the annual raise,
> vacation with pay. Want more
> of everything ready-made. Be afraid
> to know your neighbors and to die.

The imperatives sharpen the focus on what we already do. The harshness of greed seems more disturbing when it is not masked with euphemisms such as "our way of life" that elide the insidious, ever-present consequences of greed. Later in the poem he offers these homely criteria for judging the rightness of a course of action:

> Ask yourself: Will this satisfy
> a woman satisfied to bear a child?
> Will this disturb the sleep
> of a woman near to giving birth?[3]

These questions remind us of who needs protection and care, and of the investment we all have, or should have, in making the world a gentle place for women and children and for those who are vulnerable.

At the heart of many of Berry's essays are reminders of basic political principles or common ethical teachings— what was once common sense, now not so common. In *The Art of the Commonplace* he writes,

> The great enemy of freedom is the alignment of political power with wealth. This alignment destroys the commonwealth—that is, the natural wealth of localities and the local economies of household, neighborhood, and community—and so destroys democracy, of which the commonwealth is the foundation and practical means.[4]

Slightly antique words such as "commonwealth" or "proper," as in the proper use of a thing, or "conviviality," defined as "coming together with all the other creatures to the feast of Creation," remind us of the way words have been weakened by disuse or misuse and of how lovely and useful those words can be. When he says "sorrow" or "love," it is generally in a context that reminds us of the way our deepest feelings connect us with one another in the present and with the great communion of saints and ancestors who precede us.

## William Bryant Logan

The titles of Logan's books are startlingly unpretentious: *Dirt*; *Oak*; *Air*. They remind us to look and look again at what we think of as utterly ordinary features of the environment we inhabit, to recognize their complexity and their vulnerability, and to take in what they may teach us if we look at them closely enough. In *Dirt* he writes, "We spend our lives hurrying away from the real, as though it were deadly to us. 'It must be up there somewhere on the horizon,' we think. And all the time it is in the soil, right beneath our feet."[5] Like Berry, he reminds his readers of the language environment they inhabit, as well as the physical environment, and of meanings of words that have gotten lost in histories of expropriation or careless use: "In Darwin's day," he writes in *Air*, "'fittest' did not mean strongest. It meant the one that fit best into the network of mutual need."[6] That simple fact allows us to take some measure of the slippage that occurs as words are turned to purposes they weren't intended to serve. "Survival of the fittest" has a tragic history of misuse; the phrase has been expropriated by those who wanted to protect privilege by arguing that the marginalized belonged on the margins.

The whole body of Logan's work can be read as a reminder to look again at the earth we walk on, the trees that shade us, the air we breathe; to maintain our gaze long enough to take in the complexity and richness of what might seem cheap and disposable; and to learn and use words accurately, poetically, and even reverently in our conversations about the natural world, so that we neither sentimentalize nor take for granted the marvels we live among.

## Arundhati Roy

Probably best known for her novel *The God of Small Things*, Arundhati Roy has offered the world a voice and perspective from India that people in the United States especially need to hear. She is an astute observer of political and social forces that shape the lives of ordinary people as well as a writer who gives the most prosaic topics a poetic dimension. At every turn she reminds us that if something has importance it deserves to be said with clarity, accuracy, elegance, and wit. In *The Cost of Living*, for instance, one of several collections of essays and reflections, she reminds us of our common purpose in simple, elegant terms:

> To love. To be loved. To never forget your own insignificance. To never get used to the unspeakable violence and the vulgar disparity of life around you. To seek joy in the saddest places. To pursue beauty to its lair. To never simplify what is complicated or complicate what is simple. To respect strength, never power. Above all, to watch. To try and understand. To never look away. And never, never to forget.[7]

We've probably heard each of these admonitions before, many times. Hearing them again, in a simple list, without elaboration, hearing them punctuated by the word "never," gives them a new currency and urgency. The list is a distillation of wisdom with ancient history and wide resonance. It is threaded with paradox: "joy in the saddest places," beauty that lurks in a lair, strength that has nothing to do with power. It invites us to make careful distinctions, to rise above norms we live by and look from a different altitude at the terms of the lives we get, and, above all, to remember what we know.

Most children are told at some point by a disappointed parent, "You know better." We do. We know better. We need to be reminded of that.

4

## *Embrace Your Allusive Impulses*

A llusions—"indirect or passing references" to people or events, works of art or music or literature, great speeches or shared memories—can be annoying gestures of one-upmanship designed to show off one's erudition or wide reading. Even when that's not the intention, they can backfire: an editor once acerbically reminded me that not many of my readers were likely to have shared my delight in, or even recognize a reference to, a speech in an obscure play written for a rather limited audience in the 1940s, which one wouldn't likely come upon even in an English course. I left it out. Still, allusions are almost inevitable among those who read, watch movies, think about history, went to Sunday School, or paid even moderate attention in high school English.

Invoking Aristotle or Shakespeare or Abraham Lincoln or Frederick Douglass or Eleanor Roosevelt can, of course, be as manipulative as a fake reference letter when we imply perfect alignment between our point of view and those of the authorities we cite, many of whom did a good deal more homework than some of us, and paid a higher price (though to borrow from them is to let them continue to teach us). Allusions to fictional characters—Gandalf or Sherlock or Spock, for instance—shift the conversation into a space of shared story and situate us as fellow readers or viewers, fans together who may have more in common than we had imagined.

Allusions appear in various discursive environments. They lend dignity, weightiness, or irony to book titles: *A Trojan Horse in the City of God*, for instance, or *The Girl Who Takes an Eye for an Eye*, or *Blessed Are the Misfits*, or *A Rosenberg by Any Other Name*. They appear regularly in poetry; poets can hardly help borrowing or stealing as they reach for words whose singular histories and resonance they count on for their fresh purposes: "liquefaction" or "star-crossed" or "darkling." They, of all people, know that no word comes without layers of earlier context. So in a powerful poem about a friend dying of cancer, Jewish poet Chana Bloch draws richly on the biblical stories with which, as a translator of biblical material, she is deeply familiar:

> He is scooping sweetness from the belly of
> death—
> —honey from the lion's carcass.[1]

The story of Samson, legendary strong man and man of faith, hovers in the background, giving dimension to the story of a neighbor joining friends for breakfast, living his dying with courage.

Lucille Clifton makes a whole poem, "Sorrow Song," out of searing allusions to sites of atrocity that children have had to witness, each one unique in its horror, all of them also alike, the whole list together inviting us to deepen our collective determination never to see these things happen again:

> for the lingering
> eyes of the children, staring,
> the eyes of the children of
> buchenwald,
> of viet nam and johannesburg,
> for the eyes of the children
> of nagasaki,
> for the eyes of the children
> of middle passage,
> for cherokee eyes, ethiopian eyes,
> russian eyes, american eyes[2]

Rhythm or cadence as a form of allusion is subtler than direct quotation or phrases or even single words (such as "liquefaction," for example, which hardly makes sense without at least a trace memory of Robert Herrick's "On Julia's Clothes"). But allusion by sound can be the more powerful, since the sense of the past it conveys dawns on the reader or hearer more gradually. Walt Whitman made liberal use of recognizable rhythms of Jesus's words from the King James Version: "Behold me where I pass, hear my voice, approach, / Touch me, touch the palm of your hand to my body as I pass, / Be not afraid of my body."[3] He echoed biblical parallelism in pronouncements like this one to "workingmen" about bibles and religions: "It is not they who give the life, it is you who give the life."[4]

Allusiveness as a rhetorical technique, a favorite of politicians and pastors, serves to associate speakers with sources their audiences will revere. Lincoln's Second Inaugural Address, for instance, echoes Jesus in his warning about the "woe due to those by whom the offence came," echoes St. Paul in encouraging his hearers to "finish the work we are in," and marks the occasion as a sacred moment by calling upon his audience to care for the widow and the orphan. It is hardly possible to reduce Lincoln's use of this well-known rhetorical device to mere rhetorical device; rather, putting it to its best use, he invites us all to reach into the trove of collective memory for the wisdom we desperately need and, seeking it, find it—a living word that links past to present.

The reasons to include ancestors and elders in conversations that matter are more compelling than ever as historians and teachers testify to a deepening atrophy of the historical understanding we need to protect us against the debris of idle chatter and whipping winds of doctrine that are blowing all around us. Martin Luther King knew this as well as any speaker of his generation. His famous "I Have a Dream" speech is riddled with phrases from well-known hymns and songs, from the Declaration of Independence and the Constitution, and, most frequently, from the biblical prophecies and Psalms. "We shall not be satisfied," he declares, until "justice rolls down like waters, and righteousness like a mighty stream." He appeals to his hearers to "lift our nation from the quicksands of racial injustice to the solid rock of brotherhood." He begins with the phrase "five score years ago," invoking one of the most moving moments in American public history with those few words.

It takes grace and generosity to use allusions well. You have to be willing for people not to recognize them. You have to know why you're calling on Ezekiel or Emerson or Emily Brontë—for their authority? Their appeal to the imagination? Their shock value? For language lost to common use that makes us take some measure of our own usage? You have to avoid the temptation to use them to show off your own erudition. You have to be aware of what memories you evoke and what values you endorse when you quote Macbeth or Oedipus or St. Paul or Emily Dickinson. Horror at vaulting ambition? A sense of human impotence? Sure and certain hope? Delight in acid wit? You have to be aware of the original context—how an earlier audience might have thought of witches who chanted, "Double, double, toil and trouble," or what Henry David Thoreau might have seen as "lives of quiet desperation," or what it meant in 1941 to hear FDR's assurance against the backdrop of airborne bombs over England, to articulate the "four freedoms" that needed protection in time of war.

Allusiveness can add not only historical depth but live-liness, scope, irony, poignancy, creative tension, or hospi-tality to an ordinary conversation. A friend of mine had a lovely, gracious way of "reminding" us of a line she loved from Robert Frost or a striking image from one of Toni Morrison's novels or the surly way one of Flannery O'Con-nor's characters expressed herself. In case we had not in fact read the material in question, she always worked in enough context—sometimes in a subordinate clause—to help readers appreciate the point. ("These roads are di-verging," she might say of a looming decision, "and, like Frost, I'm 'sorry I cannot travel both.'") It was as though she had suddenly invited those writers into the conversation. They had something to tell us. Her shared appreciation felt like an invitation to go back and look again (or for the first time) at poems or stories that might speak to me in new ways—or sometimes to listen to a piece of music or con-sider a painting for the same reason. Allusiveness was, in her case, simply a way of being; she read widely and with an open heart and ear for a telling phrase, and it came quite naturally to her to quote phrases and lines by way of illus-trating her own fine thoughts.

Sometimes allusions provide a depth dimension so subtle it may go almost unnoticed, and yet shift the terms of the conversation and take the participants into wider waters. If I use the phrase "an eye for an eye" in a conver-sation about current disputes, I remind myself and oth-ers to remember the long course of legal history even as we wrestle with very current questions about crime and punishment. If I echo Sojourner Truth's question, "Ain't I a woman?," I conjure the memory of a freedom fighter whose story we can't afford to forget. If I observe how "the dogs go on with their doggie life," even if my hearers haven't read W. H. Auden, I've pointed the way to a poem worth reading, should they find their curiosity piqued.

Allusions are not only for public use. I was recently moved by posts a grieving father wrote for a circle of friends shortly after his beloved daughter died, leaving a sorrowing family and a bereft husband to finish the journey they had begun together. He alluded to Ophelia's "rosemary for remembrance," to a poem by Walt Whitman, to a sonnet by C. S. Lewis, and to gospel promises of eternal life. He was an English professor, so these references came quite naturally to him. But to use them, graciously, organically, poignantly, for his own present purposes was to reclaim them for all of us who read them, and to model the way our private griefs can find expression and some solace in the griefs others have felt and inscribed over time.

If allusiveness has value, of course, it has to be a two-way street. If one of my students alludes to lyrics from a song by Cardi B or Chance the Rapper, admitting my general ignorance and asking to hear the song can open conversations I might not otherwise know how to initiate; it's been a long time since Leonard Cohen and Bob Dylan and Joni Mitchell gave my generation their own ways of walking through social confusion or generational tensions or war.

Allusion at its best is an act of stewardship. Keeping ancient voices in the conversation, keeping good poems or plays or passages in public consciousness, lifting up word choices or images worthy of our notice, lifting up life-giving lines as a way of giving a breath of life, sharing the sheer deliciousness of a surprising turn of phrase—all of this can keep us all at the table together, or perhaps at a copious buffet, sharing the feast of what Matthew Arnold called "the best that has been thought and said."

Let's turn now to four allusions worth noticing.

### Your Shadow in the Land

> ... allow
> that I might glimpse once more
> Your shadow in the land ...
> —From Scott Cairns, "A Song of Isaak,
> accompanied by Jew's Harp"

"Shadow" is a loaded word; it comes with a long history, from the psalmist's "valley of the shadow of death" (Ps. 23:4 RSV) and Job's insistence that "our days on earth are but a shadow" (Job 8:9) to the humble prayer, "hide me in the shadow of your wings" (Ps. 17:8), where there is needed rest to be found in "the shadow of the Almighty" (Ps. 91:1). Carl Jung's very particular understanding of the shadow as a hidden dimension of the psyche has infused the word with psychological complexity. The long-running 1937 radio drama entitled *The*

*Shadow* popularized the ominous reminder, "Who knows what evil lurks in the hearts of men? The Shadow knows."

So this speaker's prayer for a glimpse of God's "shadow in the land" carries with it a rich ambiguity: we are neither worthy nor capable of facing God directly, but we may find refuge and safety in the shadow of the Almighty. We live with our own shadow sides, mystified by the Almighty Unknown. On the other hand, the shadow of the Divine that lies across the land brings, as the poem later says, "the sense / of dire Presence in the pulsing / hollow near the heart." Most of us want, and don't want, to experience the nearness of God. Like so many God-stricken men and women in the Bible, we are inclined to hide from the Almighty, only to find that that same God is our hiding place.

The word itself calls us back to this double-edged awareness: we rest in, and cannot escape, the shadow of the Divine that stretches across all of creation—our shade, our shelter, the veil that protects us even as it encloses us in the long valley we walk through on a path that leads to, or through, death. We are reminded by a single word that we don't get to be glib about God.

**The Word Made Flesh**

> The word, unutterably, made flesh:
> Fingers flutter, hover, fold . . .
>
> > —From Michael Cleary,
> > "Fingers, Fists, Gabriel's Wings"

The words of John 1:14, "The Word became flesh and dwelt among us," lie at the heart of the Christian story. Early in the unfolding of that story Paul assures believers that they are members of Christ's body (1 Cor. 12:27). Incarnation—embodiment—is a core idea: word and flesh become one. So in Michael Cleary's poem, in which a speaker marvels at how his words are made flesh in the skilled hands of a signer and at how those words come alive for a deaf girl, the idea of "word made flesh," borrowed from the most exquisitely poetic gospel, comes poignantly alive, and the beauty of what "blooms" in the interpreter's hands may be seen as having far more than practical value. The allusion invites us to see with reverence what comes alive and becomes transformative in the way some human found to reach beyond a barrier of disability to make a life-giving connection.

## Tiananmen Square

> It's coming through a hole in the air,
> from those nights in Tiananmen Square.
> —From Leonard Cohen, "Democracy"

The painful irony of Cohen's refrain, "Democracy is coming to the USA," deepens as the sixty-seven-line poem makes its way through multiple allusions to the history of US colonization, racism, militarism, abusive privilege, and hate. These opening lines allude to 1989 pro-democracy protests in Beijing's Tiananmen Square, the site on which Mao Tse-tung proclaimed the establishment of the People's Republic of China in 1949. Many Americans associate the name with the image of a single unidentified protestor, widely known as "Tank Man," who stood in front of tanks to stop them as they rolled through the square to stop the protests.

To Americans who invest their collective sense of national identity in the notion that we are and have been a "democratic" nation, the allusion packs a hard punch: Why would we need democracy to "come," and especially from such a place as China? The single allusion challenges a whole body of national mythology. It implies that the democracy we need may come from the least expected, and even despised, sources—from places and people to whom white North Americans have been conditioned to feel superior. Cohen's introduction of this name in this context recasts a whole orthodoxy in a single line, for those who have ears to hear and are willing to remember.

## Gandhi's Spinning Wheel

> If only Gandhi's spinning wheel had spun
> a million yards of cloth
> we would have covered all our war dead.
> —From Raza Ali Hasan,
> "In That Part of the World"

In this poem about the dead in the long war in Afghanistan, the wrenching allusion to Gandhi's spinning wheel, symbol of the simplicity of his foreshortened life, gives us a tragic sense of history. Though Gandhi has become an iconic figure and a reference point among those who advocate nonviolent peacemaking, violence has escalated steadily since his martyrdom in 1948. Even his heroic efforts weren't enough to stop the tide of war. Commitment, spiritual leadership, labor—spinning, spinning the cloth he wore to signify his identification with those whose civil rights had been systematically abridged by the caste system—weren't enough to save the next generation from violence. But to remember Gandhi in the midst of perpetual war-making is to be reminded that each generation needs someone to keep the spinning wheel going—and the peacemaking.

5

## *Tell It "Slant"*

Tell all the truth," Emily Dickinson writes, "but tell it slant." By "slant" I imagine Dickinson was referring primarily to the strategies served by poetic devices—in her case subversive, elusive, and riddled with booby traps for flat-footed literalists (not unlike some of Jesus's strategies in encounters with Pharisees: Give Caesar what is Caesar's and God what is God's. You figure out which is which). Satirists, humorists, and even scientists invite the willing and the unsuspecting to consider what they need to know from an untried angle. Finding a new angle becomes a matter of urgency when the spun and sponsored vantage points from which we are conditioned to view public events become normative. That there are other sides or more nuanced approaches to arguments for an oil pipeline or stories about drug traffickers or justifications for lucrative wars may seem obvious, but it takes vigilance, imagination, and audacity to tell them. It's hard not to fall into the grooves provided by ubiquitous repetition of words that frame what we see and obscure, often deliberately, what lies just outside the frame they establish.

Slant of some kind, of course, is inevitable. You see, and say what you see, from the angle of vision your situation provides—your family culture, your social niche, your needs, your educational conditioning, your temperament. Like a pitched ball, your words reach me in both expected (reassuring) and unexpected (unsettling) ways. Even those I know best surprise me now and then with their "way of putting it." To the extent that slant is bias, and unjust, it needs correction. But when it supplements, complements, or corrects conventions that have normalized bias, it provides a lively and necessary corrective to conventions that need to be broken up periodically like mental and cultural log jams.

I think of a story my husband tells about seeing, in the studio of a bold and remarkable artist, an oversized image of a housefly. His first reaction was what one might expect: Why would someone want to paint—or hang—an image of a housefly that would take over a whole wall? (One might wonder, of course, whether some wry play on the idea of a "fly on the wall" was involved in the artist's choice of subject.) When he wandered back for a second long look, however, he began to notice how elegant each brushstroke was. He compared the strokes to those of brush calligraphy, noticing where the brush had lifted, how subtly edges and endings called attention to the beauty of the medium itself and to the delicacy of technique. Suddenly it wasn't "just" a fly, but an ordinary, annoying, ugly insect lifted into a new kind of visibility to be seen in new terms, its intricate, iridescent, translucent complexity—its worthiness, in a sense—made available. The artist had "told the truth" about the fly in a way that lifted that fly into a place of appreciability, allowing it, in its insect way, to attest to the dignity of all being.

Like the five blind men in the old tale who take hold of different parts of the elephant and, grasping those, presume they know what an elephant is like, we need guides (and sometimes need to be the guides) who help us find our way around the body of the elephant, touching it in different places, to complicate our sense of what it is. A good jazz musician can help us hear an old song in a new and invigorating way. A good storyteller can make an ordinary trip to the grocery store into an entertaining episode. A thoughtful observer can help us imagine from a new angle another person's struggle or anxiety or pain or hope. As long as we don't assume our "slant" on things is the whole truth, and as long as we understand our purposes in putting a particular slant on the story, we can give a true account of our square foot of the elephant with integrity, and without bias.

Slant is not the same as bias. Telling truth "slant" is a way of enabling others to hear it. Emily Dickinson's insistence that "the truth must dazzle gradually" is not simply a judgment on the imaginative limitations of her reading audience, but an echo, perhaps, of Jesus's gentle reminders to his disciples that they were not ready to have all things revealed to them—that they were on a learning curve and simply didn't yet have the equipment to grasp more of the truth than their religious and cultural paradigm allowed for. He taught by indirection, intimation, riddles, suggestions, and shocking moments of revelation that left them shaken. That same understanding of how necessary it is to tailor the truth to the capacities of the hearer emerges in T. S. Eliot's "East Coker," where the speaker—or possibly a voice the speaker is channeling—advises, "Wait without hope, / for hope would be hope for the wrong thing," and further, "Wait without thought, for you are not ready for thought."[1] Most spiritual traditions teach some version of Paul's metaphorical wisdom that those who are not yet weaned are not ready for meat—that people have to grow into truth.

It can, of course, be presumptuous and dangerous to assume that any one of us is in a position to judge what our hearers or readers are capable of or ready for. All we can honestly do is offer what we see from where we stand, acknowledging the limits of our visual field, but also offering the particular insights that may be obtainable only from that particular place on earth. At the same time, we are not simply innocent reporters of what we see. Any time we string a sentence together we make strategic decisions; it's useful, effective, and right to make those decisions shrewdly.

"Shrewd" isn't a pleasant word; it sounds like "shrew,"

and originally it meant "cursed" or "wicked." From there it evolved as a descriptor for those who were "artful, tricky, or cunning." It eventually widened to the more value-neutral "showing clever resourcefulness in practical matters." One source includes the synonym "streetwise." The NIV New Testament offers as an alternative translation of the familiar line "Therefore be wise as serpents and harmless as doves" this surprising version: "Therefore be as shrewd as snakes and as innocent as doves." If we apply this to the matter of how we choose to speak or write, we have to reckon with the fact that no word choice is neutral; sometimes a single word can awaken or alienate or stop hearers in their tracks. To choose wisely or "shrewdly" is to develop some sensitivity to audiences' needs, sensitivities, expectations, fears, and usages. Jesus's parables, Hasidic tales, and myths and folktales from many traditions frequently feature characters who trick people into recognizing inconvenient truths. Shakespeare's fools operate in a similar fashion, speaking truth to power in ways that play at the outer edge of acceptability, sometimes risking the king's wrath and their own lives to speak that truth. Their saving graces are wit, edgy humor, verbal agility, astute understanding of the king's weaknesses, and, beneath all that, a large, motivating compassion that makes them able to take those risks.

Good diplomats, lawyers, negotiators, mediators, teachers, preachers, and parents take calculated risks as well, to serve the greater good. "Telling it slant," they bypass defenses and find their way into the risky intimacy that honest confrontation requires. They learn, for example, to reframe a cost as a savings; a loss as a lesson; a forfeiture as a fair exchange; a sacrifice as a route to joy; a disappointment as a moment of opportunity and growth. We can all tell when such reframings are cheap or disingenuous, but when they come from authentic concern for our well-being, when they trick us into truth, we end up grateful.

Most tribal stories include some version of the "trickster" archetype. Tricksters are, as Lewis Hyde put it in *Trickster Makes This World*, "boundary-crossers."[2] They challenge social norms, mock authority, laugh in the "wrong" places, outwit conventional rule followers, and defy categories. Sometimes they are shape shifters or "gender benders." Sometimes they challenge heroes in ways that enable them to rise to their tasks. Sometimes they turn out to be the heroes. The Greek god Hermes is a trickster, as are the Norse god Loki, and Coyote in Native American tales, and Br'er Rabbit, and Aesop's fox. The stories of Jacob in the Old Testament depict him as a trickster, as when he tricks Esau out of his inheritance. And Jesus himself, when he is deft and witty and elusive in his exchanges with the ruling elders of his community, assumes the same role. Tricksters enter the stage from odd angles, take us by surprise, catch us off guard, and throw us off balance, all in the service of a truth that can't be seen clearly through the lenses cultural conventions provide. They keep us awake when we'd rather sleep. They needle us into knowing what we'd rather not know. They lead us to laugh in the face of our most paralyzing fears. We need them for sanity and self-correction. Sometimes we need to be them.

Satire is a form of "slant" we are familiar with in contemporary comedy. Historically, satire tends to proliferate when cultures or civilizations are in decline, when leadership is corrupt, when corruptions and injustices have been normalized or even become normative, and when the needs of the people go unmet. Good satirists sidestep direct confrontation and manage to avoid being silenced or punished by switching genres: if news reporting and analysis airs on Comedy Central or comes dressed as a skit on *Saturday Night Live*, those who deliver it can generally, like Lear's fool, speak truth to power by posting images and posing questions that expose their absurdities. Ultimately, their aim is to restore order of a different kind—order that is not the status quo, but that reestablishes justice, equity, clarity, and compassion for those who have no voice. Satire, though it has its own abuses and may degenerate into cheap sarcasm, at its best offers us a back road by which to find our way to truth.

Examples of good satire abound now, as public discourse becomes dominated by slurs and slogans and as the lip service paid to checks and balances, human rights, and economic equity wears thin. Those among us who "tell it slant" often bring us the prophetic word we need in a time of great trouble. Let's consider five examples of writers and public figures whose slant on the big questions of our time and culture open windows we need on landscapes we might otherwise miss.

## David Quammen

Quammen, one of my favorite popular science writers, makes good use of slant. One of his early books, *Natural Acts*, is subtitled *A Sidelong View of Science and Nature*.[3] The essays in it include one that invites us to consider what happens when you make eye contact with a spider, one that directs our attention to the fate of urban trees, and one that poses the curious question whether success has "spoiled the crow."

One of Quammen's abiding concerns is loss of species habitats and consequent loss of species and then of the biodiversity that insures a healthy planet. He writes about the way humans are contributing to cataclysmic extinction rates by destroying ecosystems. He writes about dire, even apocalyptic things. His pleas for species preservation are liberally seasoned with a humor that enables even reluctant readers to consider deeply troubling issues with activated concern rather than paralyzing angst. He connects widely dispersed dots among philosophy, art, and ecology in a piece entitled "Jeremy Bentham, the *Pietà*, and Precious Few Greyling" to persuade readers to care for apparently un-useful species.

Quammen's degree is in English, not biology. He presents living testimony to the fact that all of us who hope to be effective citizens and morally responsible human beings need some understanding of biology, along with history, politics, and physics. He wrote two novels before he turned to zoology in what he calls his "critter column" for *Outside Magazine*. He infuses his well-turned sentences with aphorisms, oxymorons, ironic anthropomorphisms, and playful disruptions that jolt readers out of unexamined assumptions. His writing models shrewd intelligence, informed urgency, generous humor that assumes community with all his readers, an unwillingness to "suffer fools gladly," and always an element of surprise that jars us into new awareness.

## Mary Oliver

Oliver, one of the few contemporary American poets to read to packed audiences everywhere she went in the final decades of her richly lived life, taught all of us who read her to see the natural world with fresh eyes by giving us her own "sidelong view." One of her most popular poems begins with the startling line, "You do not have to be good," and ends by directing our attention to how the world "calls to you like the wild geese, harsh and exciting, / over and over announcing your place / in the family of things."[4] The poem lifts us out of the oppressive thicket of simplistic moral self-judgment into a place of wide-angled awareness of relationship with all beings that challenges and deepens our notions of what is good or moral or right. She asks a question many have found restorative in its unusual reminder of possibility: "Tell me, what is it you plan to do / with your one wild and precious life?" That life is "wild and precious" may have escaped our notice in the course of our daily trips to work, workout, meetings, meals, and the online sites to which carefully targeted ads lead us. The natural world that she reminds us we inhabit is not shrouded in sentimentality or made to conform to our notions of what is beautiful or noble, but one we might imagine from the perspective of the vultures who "minister to the grassy miles" or the humpback whales who "throb with song."

## Nadia Bolz-Weber

Bolz-Weber has won a good bit of notoriety among contemporary Christian pastors for her edgy, in-your-face style; her occasional use of vulgar language and even profanity in sermons and speeches; her tattoos; and the church she founded, called the "House for All Sinners and Saints." She is, against all conventional appearances, a devout believer, driven by a love of God that refuses to be confused with class-bound respectability. Her "slant" delivery of the message of the gospel is remarkably orthodox, but it seeks to restore some of the shock value of Jesus's original message to the conventionally pious of his generation. Her understanding of Mary, for instance, revered and represented in so much art as quintessentially "feminine" in her submissive holiness, gives us a new angle on a woman of great faith and great courage who stood up with and to Jesus himself: "I started to imagine Mary tugging at the shirt of Jesus and saying, I will not keep silent. I will obey you and I will tell others to obey you but I will not keep silent. People are thirsty. In John's Gospel, Mary is not the young virgin pondering sweet things in her heart. In John's Gospel, Mary is not surrounded by singing angels. . . . I started to see Mary in a long line of prophets who have not kept silent. The prophet Mary stands and says, 'Lord, we've run out of wine and people are thirsty.' And Jesus hears her."[5]

## Toni Morrison

Morrison occupies a prominent and in many ways unique place among experimental novelists, African American novelists, and contemporary women writers. Her characters occupy a world where the veil is thin between natural and supernatural, and where social powerlessness and spiritual empowerment coexist in characters who defy simple classification. Readers are required to assess their own capacity to "suspend disbelief" enough to allow for ghosts, visions, telepathy, and other preternatural powers, as well as having to take full account of the extent of the abuse suffered by enslaved, exploited human beings, and with what effects. Like other African American writers, she alludes often to that history, but allows us to see it as in a curved mirror, the distortions disturbing in their deviation from what we think is "normal," but also in the way they foreground truths usually discreetly camouflaged: children learn to displace their suffering; those who have a history of suffering develop a symbolic language and rituals to allow it to be spoken of without ripping open the wounds. To read Morrison's stories is to be unsettled, disturbed into accepting things you might not even find believable, humbled by the kaleidoscopic variety of what we far too simply call good and evil.

## Leonard Cohen

In 2016 the *New York Times* ran a piece on Leonard Cohen that called him a "master of meanings and incantatory verse." One bit of description of his song lyrics also serves to describe his persona: "morbid while keeping a hint of puckishness." The writer also remembers him as "sly and avuncular, making droll, deadpan comments in his sepulchral voice."[6] His words were cryptic, prophetic, precisely aimed at contemporary sensibilities, but echoes of ancient myths, biblical material, and history ironically remembered. He had a knack for making the personal political and vice versa. His words last because they are adaptable, widely applicable without losing their specificity, rich and rueful in the humane, challenging way they mirror back for us experiences lodged in collective memory that we cannot afford to forget—reminders that "Everybody knows the fight was fixed / The poor stay poor, the rich get rich, / That's how it goes / everybody knows," and that the "hallelujah" we are likely to hear is often "cold and broken." He tells truths "slant" like driven rain, and they are dark, but haunting, and gleaming with some light of truth that comes in through the "crack in everything."[7]

## *Promote Poetry*

I n an earlier book, *Caring for Words in a Culture of Lies*, I wrote a chapter entitled "Practice Poetry." This is a continuation of the conversation I began there. Poetry as a "practice" includes both reading it and writing it, recognizing it as a rich and necessary dimension of private and public conversation that we can ill afford to neglect. It's a public responsibility, not just a private practice. "Promoting" poetry means reading it aloud, with others, attending poetry readings, making room for it in periodicals and magazines and on websites and social media, normalizing it, holding it to considered standards of quality, making it part of public discourse, knowing it provides a dimension of understanding and awareness that no other form can quite provide.

In *Saved by a Poem*, testifying to the relevance, power, and urgency of poetry, Kim Rosen writes,

> In the last ten years I have spent time in refugee camps, war-torn countries, homeless shelters, pris-

ons, and post-disaster sites. Most recently I have been in the Democratic Republic of the Congo, where some of the greatest atrocities of this century are being perpetrated on the bodies of thousands of women. What form can give adequate expression to the scope of such pain? What language can invite our connection, our care, our action without compelling us to cover our ears and flee from the horror?

Poetry is the language of our time. It is a verbal excavation, digging us into and under that which is inarticulate, that which cannot be said but can be felt, that which cannot be stated but can be conjured. Poetry is a form of revolution. It rearranges our thinking, our perception, our dialogue. It takes us out of the literal so that we can see what is real.[1]

These are strong claims. I believe them. The practice of poetry, even for prose writers, even for those who write only in journals sequestered in locked drawers, invigorates the mind and keeps the heart open. Dangling out there in negative space, those words at the ends of lines make themselves heard and give us pause. The rhythms poets find, like those of jazz drummers, align our own heartbeats to others' and train sensibilities that lie just beneath our defensive intellectual radar.

The first stanza of Etheridge Knight's poem, "Hard Rock Returns to Prison from the Hospital for the Criminal Insane," for instance, prepares us to enter into deepening horror at the story of a young man subjected to shock treatment to tame him so he could go from one incarceration to another:

> Hard Rock / was / "known not to take no shit
> From nobody," and he had the scars to
>     prove it:
> Split purple lips, lumped ears, welts above
> His yellow eyes, and one long scar that cut
> Across his temple and plowed through a thick
> Canopy of kinky hair.

The last of several subsequent stanzas bears witness to what is destroyed when young men's outrage is criminalized without inquiry and punished in ways that avoid the rigors of reconciliation:

> And even after we discovered that it took
>     Hard Rock
> Exactly 3 minutes to tell you his first name,
> We told ourselves that he had just wised up,
> Was being cool; but we could not fool our-
>     selves for long,
> And we turned away, our eyes on the ground.
>     Crushed.
> He had been our Destroyer, the doer of things
> We dreamed of doing but could not bring
>     ourselves to do,

*Promote Poetry*

> The fears of years, like a biting whip,
> Had cut deep bloody grooves
> Across our backs.[2]

These are hard truths. They're hard lines. They're jag-ged. They speak about pain, and they're painful to read. They're alternately jarring, confessional, poignant, and coolly informative. Those of us who practice poetry in rel-atively peaceful places—classrooms, writing groups, and cluttered studies—need to keep an ear open for the poetry that comes from streets where it is fueled by a rage we can't afford to dismiss, not because it is dangerous, but because it is a life force.

Poets occupy their own space in public argument. They may seem marginal to those looking for crisp, informative news updates, but the genre itself is a powerful tool that can widen and fine-tune our awareness of what we're wit-nessing in the world around us. We rely on poets to resist, or at least offer an alternative to, media-speak, corporate discourse, and journalism that has been diminished by in-cessant and increasing haste.

Poetry, of course, is "slant" by nature. It disrupts syn-tax, breaks lines in odd places, defeats left-brain logic, and makes uncommon sense. That's one of the best reasons to read it: because it calls a rose by another name and shows us a road less traveled and won't let literal dogs lie and leans a little to one side. A friend recently sent me a pho-tograph of a sign on a public thoroughfare that proclaimed in large capital letters, "There must be more poetry." Oppressed people know this, and poets are popular heroes in war-torn cultures—Nizar Qabbani, for instance, considered Syria's national poet, or Ibrahim Quashoush, another Syrian poet who was abducted and killed in 2011 while two other Syrian poets were being held in prison. They, and other poets in Iraq, Afghanistan, Honduras, Eastern Europe, and other sites of ongoing conflict, realize that, as Audre Lorde put it, "poetry is not a luxury." It is an instrument of awareness and survival.

In "Poetry Diplomacy in the Congo," Annie Finch writes, "The DRC is one of the hardest places on the planet to be a woman or a poet. Terrorization through rape, child prostitution, and brutal government repression is routine. Resources are scarce to an extent that, by normal U.S. standards, is literally unbelievable . . . poets and writers have scant access to either books or publishers." And yet, they write, holding one another to standards that "put ours to shame." She goes on, "Their commitment to art is akin to that of the incredible musicians in the award-winning documentary *Kinshasa Symphony*, so dedicated to their music that they build their own instruments when necessary."[3]

Most of us in North America (though there are notable exceptions) are not driven to poetry in quite that way—in the way Auden imagined in his beautiful eulogy, "In Memory of W. B. Yeats": "Mad Ireland hurt you into poetry." But most of us venture into poetry now and then, aware that what needs to be a poem can't be anything else, that poems meet a need for both writer and reader that can't be met any other way, and that poems also meet public needs. The calling to write poetry, whether it is a lifelong vocation or simply an occasional inspiration, can serve a variety of purposes, some of which we may not even recognize when we set out to write it.

Some poets are peacemakers. They help us retrieve language that gets lost in an avalanche of political punditry, rhetorical overkill, ads, promotional copy, and slogans. Wendell Berry is one of these. He invites us to imagine "The Peace of Wild Things," or to see the forest as a "timbered choir," or to seek peace like the "Mad Farmer" by practicing quiet, persistent, inventive forms of life-affirming subversion—planting sequoias, going with our love to the fields, practicing resurrection. Mary Oliver is another; she has invited a whole generation to take another long, caring, careful look at the natural world we are so prone to squander and abuse, and to rediscover how our own life and health and happiness depend on it. She has given us questions that make us accountable in new ways, such as this one, widely applicable: "Here is a story / to break your heart. / Are you willing?"[4]

Some poets are healers; some become healers by mapping their own hard journeys with illness, disability, sorrow, and loss so that the rest of us, their readers, know, when it is our turn to enter cancer treatment or rehab or caregiving for parents with dementia or shocking bereavement, that we are not alone. Poetry by people with cancer, for instance, offers a view from inside what Susan Sontag called "the kingdom of the sick," complicating our notions about what illness and healing look like and inviting us to imagine how living, even while dying, may become "rich and strange" in new ways. Susan Spady, midway through a poem about her "asymmetrical" life after a mastectomy, poses a question that drops to a new level of philosophical reflection: "What does the body house, / except a dream of perfection? / And what houses the body?"[5] Annie Stenzel, weeks after receiving a diagnosis of multiple sclerosis, explores the nightly challenge of fear, dread, and unknowing in "An Incantation for the Small Hours of the Night":

> Unspeakable some thing is stalking me
> silent in its approach
> Indifferent some thing has me in its sights
> is circling (no malice, just menace)
> inexorable, unavoidable
> Incomprehensible some thing is there
> in the darkness beside me. . . .[6]

Mary Bradish O'Connor ends her poem "Midnight Cancer," a chronicle of the ways in which the illness intrudes on her consciousness throughout the day, with the simple, ominous lines, "It is midnight. / You have cancer." Poems like these equip patients and their caregivers. They help us imagine how to care, how to cope, how to witness what is happening from a different altitude, claiming life on new terms, not altogether disabling—sometimes empowering.

Some poets are witnesses, reporters, even occasionally prophets who speak a hard and timely truth, like Rafeef Ziadah, who responds to a reporter's simplistic request that she speak about Palestinian life without referencing politics with a poem that reiterates the simple refrain, "We teach life, sir"—an eloquent insistence that life in disputed territory, life in a time of ongoing warfare, life in a place where children die violently is, by definition, political.[7]

If each of us shared particular poems that had helped us mature in our understanding of faith or feelings or politics, that had helped us fine-tune our sense of how words resonate and ring true, that had given us moments of insight or joy or empathy, a "greening" of public space would take place, like the greening of a lawn after being seeded in spring. Here is a short list of five contemporary poems, easily located online, that deserve a wide reading for their power and relevance. There are many others. I hope they serve as an invitation to pick your own favorites and share widely.

## Ellen Bass, "Dead Butterfly"

In this short poem a mother speaks about a child who for a time carries a dead butterfly everywhere with her in a jar. The mother simply allows and wonders at the sad, inexplicable attachment, respecting the child's need or grief without probing, aware of the way it mirrors something of her own desire to carry and protect what is already beyond her protection.[8]

## Naomi Shihab Nye, "Different Ways to Pray"

In six stanzas the poet offers readers rich glimpses of Arab peasant life where prayer is threaded into daily life, its forms adapted to the tasks of those for whom work and prayer are contiguous, or calling them forth into pilgrimage and out of time. As ordinary as it is mysterious, prayer, like breathing, fuels the bodies of those who pray and sustains even the young ones who no longer do so.[9]

## Li-Young Lee, "Praise Them"

This quiet, startling meditation on what birds do as they pass among us (they "do not alter space" but "reveal it") offers a reminder to notice what gifts and lessons may be taken from the undemanding creatures whose little lives remain mysterious to us, but whose singing "completes us."[10]

## Chana Bloch, "Blood Honey"

Written before her own cancer took her generous life, this poem, mentioned above, is the poet's amazed meditation on how a friend, dying of cancer, is "scooping sweetness from the belly of death"—a reference to the biblical story of Samson scooping honey from a lion's carcass. Locating a real and present sorrow in the context of an ancient sacred tale gives the moment scope and depth and prepares a ritual place for grief at the same time that the poem offers a powerful, poignant reminder to eat that honey, living deeply into the present, tasting and seeing that, even with all its appalling darkness, "The world is good."[11]

### Debra Spencer, "At the Arraignment"

In this wry, subversive, challenging poem, Jesus appears in a courtroom with group after group of prisoners, witnessing the sentencing of people whose "crimes" are rooted in poverty and hunger. In the final stanza, Jesus addresses the other spectators, asking them, "Which of us has never broken a law?" and challenging them, "If you can't be merciful, at least be bold." It is a poem to reread and share among all who are concerned with the upstream causes of mass incarceration and a justice system in which too often justice gives way to timidity and indifference. Its surprise ending invites a radical rereading of what it might mean to practice resurrection.[12]

We need poets—those who are published and posted, those who read in local schools, those who write and post occasionally, those who carry other people's poems in their pockets to reread until they carry them in their hearts—

their courage, their clarity, their articulate compassion, the phrases and images that lay down new paths in the imagination and bring us to salutary tears or enough life-giving outrage to act.

## *Articulate Your Outrage*

Chris Hedges, Pulitzer Prize–winning journalist, graduate of Harvard Divinity School, and witness to more sorrows than most of us will see in a lifetime, has reported from war zones all over the world and placed himself many times in harm's way. The justifiable outrage that fuels much of his writing comes from a calling that has cost him dearly in personal anguish. He has earned the right to outrage—or some might say righteous anger—by risking his own life for the sake of reporting stories of suffering and reflecting on its causes, speaking forcefully against the principalities and powers that perpetuate harm. He begins a recent essay on the American media in this way:

> The press . . . chatters endlessly like 18th-century courtiers at the court of Versailles about the foibles of the monarch while the peasants lack bread. It drones on and on and on about empty topics such as Russian meddling and a payoff to a porn actress that have nothing to do with the daily hell that, for many, defines

life in America. It refuses to critique or investigate the abuses by corporate power, which has destroyed our democracy and economy and orchestrated the largest transfer of wealth upward in American history. The corporate press is a decayed relic that, in exchange for money and access, committed cultural suicide.[1]

It might seem to some that these forthright accusations come at the cost of civility. Reading Hedges and others who write and speak on matters of public urgency that need more of a hearing than they're getting makes me wonder if there aren't times to reexamine and perhaps redefine civility. If the facts have been checked, and if they deserve urgent attention, an outcry may be called for. Hedges writes about the world he inhabits with the weight of experience few of us would envy and an unflinching view of institutions won at great cost. If we haven't done the homework, we have little right to accuse and call to account. If we have, we may find ourselves called to do exactly that.

It is a call that demands careful discernment; it is perilously easy to persuade ourselves that our own anger is righteous. Hedges's reference to the "corporate press" as a "decayed relic" that "chatters" and "drones" is not an invitation to academic reflection about the nature of news. Rather, it is a call to intelligent action; it is a call to dissent and disobedience as a way of protecting an institution we all depend on for accurate information upon which we can stake our health and safety, our investments and votes and daily decisions. Some public crises in our time, he believes, have reached a threat level beyond the possibility of meaningful compromise. He has the facts to focus his anger. He invites us, as Paul puts it, to be angry with a kind of anger that is not sin, but energized compassion—compassion on fire.

Hedges has counterparts in every arena of public life: Cornel West takes on white supremacy with similar force when he speaks of the "degradation of black bodies in order to control them,"[2] and of institutionalized ways to terrorize people that begin simply by convincing them that they are stupid, ugly, and uncivilized. Michelle Alexander, in *The New Jim Crow,* writes in a similar vein,

> We use our criminal justice system to label people of color "criminals" and then engage in all the practices we supposedly left behind. Today it is perfectly legal to discriminate against criminals in nearly all the ways that it was once legal to discriminate against African Americans. Once you're labeled a felon, the old forms of discrimination—employment discrimination, housing discrimination, denial of the right to vote, denial of educational opportunity, denial of food stamps and other public benefits, and exclusion from jury service—are suddenly legal. As a criminal, you have scarcely more rights, and arguably less respect, than a black man living in Alabama at the height of Jim Crow. We have not ended racial caste in America; we have merely redesigned it.[3]

It is still neither easy nor entirely safe for a person of color in this country to speak truth to or about those who wield power and often abuse it. Many who do are caught in a double bind: if they do not speak, they betray suffering people; if they do, they may forfeit hard-won access to those in a position to bring about change.

Public outrage is costly. You do lose some of your audience: you offend some; you scare some away; you're labeled, often inaccurately, and pigeonholed; you find yourself with strange bedfellows whose positions or purposes may be only tangentially related to your own. And yet, we need the energy of outrage on occasion, and of those who are willing to articulate it—not the spluttering of well-paid pundits, but the focused force of clear, accurate naming of what is happening. We see this kind of articulation in the prophet Jeremiah, who, delivering God's warnings to Israel, cries, "I am full of the wrath of the Lord; I am weary of holding it in" (Jer. 6:11). The verb is significant: we speak of "holding our peace," meaning refraining from speaking out unless and until the time is right. But what we hold when we do that—what we hold in, in order to hold peace—may become too weighty or too pressing to contain. When children are being slaughtered or wrenched away from their families, when girls are being sold into sex slavery, when the wealthy are being enriched by exploitation of the laboring poor, when noncombatants are wantonly killed, when people are mocked or marginalized or shamed or harmed—we need to be sure we don't mistake timidity for civility.

*Articulate Your Outrage*

Civility is a public virtue. Its root, *civitas*—city—reminds us that we exercise that virtue for the common good. When the common good is served by holding our peace while someone with whom we disagree has a chance to be heard, the civil hold their peace. When the common good is served by speaking out with vigor, candor, directness, and urgency, the civil speak out. They speak for. And they know whereof they speak. Civility and outrage are no strangers to each other. Consider, for example, the long list of serious grievances leveled at the king of England in the Declaration of Independence. The colonists were fed up with a system of taxation without representation, of obstructions of justice, delays and deferrals, invasive and unequal treatment of English citizens in America, and a host of other inequities. The document begins courteously, pointing out that it sometimes "becomes necessary" for one people to "dissolve the political bands which have connected them with another," invoking the "laws of Nature and Nature's God" as the authorizing power that underwrites their complaints. The long list of outrages following that famously measured prologue is no rant; it is a list of twenty-seven specific facts "summoned to a candid world" to prove their case against the king. As the facts accumulate, the injustice of British policies becomes more starkly apparent. The writers appeal to common sense in a common cause: "repeated injuries and usurpations" need to be named, challenged, and resisted.

Those challenges need to be made, often, on behalf of

those who have no access to the public forum. The men who met in Philadelphia in 1776 were landowners—not all wealthy, but all men of privilege—who had an eye, no doubt, on their own long-term interests, though they were risking their lives to put their names on that document. But they also levied their complaints on behalf of small farmers and indentured servants and children born to immigrants and those fleeing persecution. Though they were imperfect and prejudiced, their outrage rested on concern for the public and for posterity. And that seems one of several important litmus tests for legitimate outrage: that one's concern must extend beyond personal affront.

As we determine whether to take our anger on the road, it's good to ask ourselves a few test questions:

1) What am I hoping to protect?
2) What principle is at stake?
3) Am I the most appropriate person to step into this ring?
4) What am I risking?
5) What makes it worth the risk?
6) Is this the moment?
7) What would be the consequences of holding my peace?

Sometimes, as many a courageous leader has pointed out, silence is cowardly complicity or worse. Gandhi, for instance, put it fairly simply: "Silence becomes cowardice when occasion demands speaking out the whole truth and acting accordingly." And Martin Luther King's eloquent echo reinforces that indictment: "Our lives begin to end the day we become silent about things that matter." Both men spent long periods of their public lives in silence, waiting for the moment to speak. Both spoke when they determined those moments had come. Both died for it. The cost of articulating our outrage may be high. It may be required of us.

In his little book *On Tyranny: Twenty Lessons from the Twentieth Century*, historian Timothy Snyder urges, among other strategies for avoiding predictable patterns of capitulation to corrupt power, that we not make a habit of needless (or mindless) obedience, that we be willing to "stand out," that we "make eye contact" with others to resist a climate of fear, that we "listen for dangerous words," and finally that we be courageous, because courage will be required.[4] It always has been required of those who seek to live with integrity. The book is a timely word in a world where tyrannies and oppression proliferate, but the wisdom it offers is not new; Peter's admonition in the first century has ample contemporary relevance: "Be sober, be watchful. Your adversary the devil prowls around like a roaring lion, seeking someone to devour" (1 Pet. 5:8 RSV). Watchfulness and sobriety entail a willingness to confront rather than capitulate, to cry out rather than cringe inwardly. The trick is to know when.

By way of examples, then, consider a few courageous

persons whose articulate outrage has served the public over the past couple of generations.

## W. H. Auden

This poet, known for the irony, wit, spiritual depth, and range of his poems, might seem an unlikely example of articulate outrage, but I have long appreciated exactly that gift in one of his better-known poems. "Stop All the Clocks" has been a help to me and to many others in the early stages of grief, when one feels utterly inconsolable. In a series of sharp imperatives, the speaker orders the signifiers of ordinary to be snuffed out: "cut off the telephone," "prevent the dog from barking," "silence the pianos," and later, more extravagantly, "put out" the stars, "not wanted now," "Pack up the moon and dismantle the sun."[5] The final bleak and shocking line, "For nothing now can ever come to any good," offers no consolation but that of full-bodied acknowledgment of what it feels like to be bereft. Reading it, I often think of a woman in her seventies—a woman of great faith, in fact—who, when asked at her beloved husband's funeral how she was feeling, answered simply, "I'm outraged." Death may be a surprising transition into a world of love and light, but to recognize it as a curse is the other side of the ultimate paradox. It is good to give voice to that outrage; if we do not—if we rush too quickly to consolation and omit the keening and weeping—we may forfeit the blessing due to "those who mourn" (Matt. 5:4).

## Marian Wright Edelman

Her long track record of child advocacy and activism for more adequate and equal education has justly placed Marian Wright Edelman among the elders many revere as key voices for change. She is a strong and civil speaker—forthright and measured and generous in her demeanor, but capable of igniting a blaze of righteous anger in her hearers as she details the profound inequities that disable children socially and economically, especially children of color and children of immigrants. Years ago, I heard her give one of her many stirring commencement addresses, in which her challenge to every hopeful young person there was to use their privilege for service, because otherwise their education would be a waste. "Service is the rent we pay for being," she has said on numerous occasions; "it is the very purpose of life and not something you do in your spare time." In a commencement address at UCLA, she quoted Martin Luther King's prophetic fear that the country was sowing the seeds of its own destruction through materialism, militarism, and racism and his admonishment to be among those "to sound the alarm." She underscored that urgent directive, giving full weight to the dangers we create for ourselves and offering only the final word of encouragement that we may still be able to "turn danger into hope." Like King, she embodies that hard-won hope but in no way minimizes the outrage that must be faced for hope to be authentic: the "cradle to prison pipeline"; the environments of poverty, drunkenness, and despair in which so many children have to learn to survive; the gun violence that is an ever-present threat on some streets children have to walk along on their way to school. Her writings and talks remind me repeatedly of Thomas Hardy's great observation that "if way to the better there be, it exacts a full look at the worst." Look and be outraged, she urges in one eloquent story after another. And then act.[6]

## Dietrich Bonhoeffer

Described by Victoria Barnett, director of Programs on Ethics, Religion, and the Holocaust at the United States Holocaust Memorial Museum, as "a man who tried to face the darkness of his times" with "the faith of someone who had gone through his times with his eyes wide open," Bonhoeffer has offered a pertinent model of controlled, focused, informed, purposeful outrage for both believers and nonbelievers since his death in 1945. Far from simply blaming Hitler and his inner circle for the evils of the Third Reich, though he certainly called out what there was to blame, Bonhoeffer understood how, when evil is normalized and institutionalized, everyone in the system is contaminated by complicity rooted in indifference or fear. "We are not to simply bandage the wounds of victims beneath the wheels of injustice," he wrote; "we are to drive a spoke into the wheel itself."[7] Bonhoeffer's involvement in a plot to assassinate Hitler has remained controversial among his readers and followers, but perhaps more important was his challenge to the passive complicity that made cowards of Christians whose faith had failed to take root deeply enough to withstand the seductions of safety. From prison and before then, Bonhoeffer preached against judging others—a practice that blinds us to our own evil "and to the grace which others are just as entitled to as we are." But his clarity about the difference between mercy and leniency remains a stringent reminder not to mistake timidity for patience.

## Martin Luther King

"Injustice anywhere is a threat to justice everywhere" is just one of the many memorable lines from Martin Luther King's speeches and sermons, ringing with prophetic truth that we needed then—and need now—to keep hearing. His doctrine of love never excluded outrage or anger, but it insisted that anger be transformed into action. He told a story of how having witnessed his father's anger at being sent to the back of the line in a store "played a great part in shaping" his conscience. Clarence Jones, King's attorney and speechwriter, recalled, "From Dr. King's standpoint, anger is part of a process that includes anger, forgiveness, redemption and love."[8]

Part of King's legacy lives in the so-called RULER approach to emotional regulation, developed by the Yale Center for Emotional Intelligence, which helps enable people

faced with violence and injustice to accomplish that transformation of anger into action. This training focuses on
five practical steps in redirecting the energy of anger into
fruitful protest and articulate advocacy:

1) Recognize the anger many people across the nation
   share.
2) Understand that anger is a likely response to wit-
   nessing or experiencing injustice.
3) Label anger and other emotions accurately.
4) Express the anger in helpful, rather than hurtful
   ways (remember who you're speaking for, not just
   what you're speaking against).
5) Regulate emotions to transform anger into peaceful
   and powerful action.

It is hard to do any of these things alone. Discernment and
practical decision-making need to take place in groups
where encouragement, reiteration of common purposes,
and informed direction can take place in a safe space.

## Sherman Alexie

One of a rising number of Native American storytellers
who funnel their wit, intelligence, and rage against injustice into stories and poems, novels, plays, and performance
events, Alexie has held the distinction for some time of
being among the most controversial of these writers. His

childhood and youth on a reservation gave him his recurrent themes of despair, poverty, violence, and alcoholism, but also the resilient wit of a trickster and the courage of one who has seen behind masks of power and privilege and knows the latent power that resides in the underestimated masses of the marginalized. When Arizona excised his works from school curricula by law, he responded with invigorating defiance:

> I'm . . . strangely pleased that the folks of Arizona have officially announced their fear of an educated underclass. You give those brown kids some books about brown folks and what happens? Those brown kids change the world. In the effort to vanish our books, Arizona has actually given them enormous power. Arizona has made our books sacred documents now.[9]

Outrage like Alexie's can (and often does) look like arrogance or officiousness or, certainly, impropriety. But it can be what fuels love of justice and mercy and, finally, a humility that survives humiliation.

8

## *Find Facts and Check Them*

Naomi Klein has written courageous and, some would say, prophetic books on sweat shops, economic inequities, and climate change. She can give a pretty accurate account of the dollar cost of the Tar Sands pipeline. She bothered to find out and record the fact that in 2007 the three major networks ran 147 stories on climate change, and that in 2010 that number had dropped to 32. And she's good at putting those numbers together with a good many others and taking a hard look at their implications. She has survived efforts to debunk her claims by passing through the fine filters of experienced fact-checkers like Mike Caulfield. More than an investigative reporter or an economist, Klein—like Bill McKibben, Chris Hedges, Amy Goodman, Jeremy Scahill, Robert Fisk, and thousands of their unsung colleagues—writes and speaks about some of the most threatening and controversial events of our time as an ally of the poor, a citizen of the earth, and a steward of its gifts. The facts she marshals and documents gather into strong patterns of evidence as she laces them with dates, every date invoking her readers' recent memories of public events that she helps reinterpret in light of economic realities that are often carefully shielded or spun to prevent exactly what she's doing. She makes no facile accusations, but she does make some informed ones, stripping the sheep's clothing away from the naked greed that often shapes economic policies and trade agreements.

Like Klein, Harvey Wasserman, a writer who has devoted much of his working life to opposing nuclear proliferation and promoting renewable energy, defends the vulnerable who live near nuclear waste dumps and other forms of outsourced pollution, not only by teaching citizens to advocate for themselves and for the common good, but also by doing the same kind of due diligence Klein does, to similar powerful effect. Here's a paragraph about the nuclear meltdown at Fukushima. Note the teacherly clarity and care with which each fact and its implications are presented:

> We have to understand about these rods, by the way. They are the most lethal substance human beings have ever created. If a rod had been in this room when we started this interview, we'd be all dead by now. It is incredibly toxic stuff. In addition to that, the fuel rods are clad in zirconium alloy. Zirconium alloy will spontaneously ignite if it's exposed to air. That's why it has to be kept under water at all times. Zirconium is actually the element that was used in those old flash

cubes that burnt so bright so quickly when you took a photograph in the old days. So this zirconium alloy is incredibly dangerous . . . ; it needs to be kept cool 100% underwater or it will ignite, and it burns very hot and could in fact cause the fuel rods to catch fire.[1]

The best nonfiction writers and public speakers understand their work as public service. They do homework—a lot of it. They cross-check. Though they use words that end in "ism," they're much more likely to use words like "oil," "carbon," "permafrost," "zirconium," "depleted uranium," "wounds," "civilians," and "drones." Or "food stamps," "prescription drugs," and "eviction notice." They like concrete nouns and verbs. These words are not ideological terms, though some dispute the conclusions they draw from the evidence they provide. But taking responsibility for providing evidence and also for explaining their inferences keeps the invitation open to those willing to do the same.

Any earnest student will tell you it's hard to find and trust facts these days. Accusations of bias fly around like spores in the wind, and almost any source is likely to be tarred with a partisan brush. A growing number of common words—"gun," "immigrant," "welfare," "choice," "family," "evangelical," "justice," "protest," "climate"—have become triggers: it is hard to nuance arguments in which they have already set off hearers' or readers' early warning systems. For that reason, we need people who speak and write to find real facts in the mire of abstractions that are the common currency of political debate and to check and double-check and cross-check those facts. Fortunately, some websites still have wide, though not universal, credibility as places where facts can be checked. Factcheck.org, Politifact, Snopes, Truth Be Told, and Guardian Reality Check are helpful. So are the circles of trust we inhabit: I have come to rely on certain friends who do the deep reading and research required to provide accurate readings of complicated current issues. One can tell me any time I ask what is happening between Israel and Palestine, offering particulars, gathered from multiple sources he has come to trust, that humanize and clarify what is happening on the ground. Another knows a great deal about the American medical system and how different insurance plans work. She knows in usable detail why one plan might be better for a particular family than another. She can help frame the questions that enable less informed people to navigate vast medical bureaucracies. Another is deeply informed about the food system—where decisions are made for grocery chains, what fast-food production has meant for rain forests and potato farming and schools, what happens in factory farms, what nutritional facts are most important to know. All of them pay attention to particulars.

A verifiable fact is a treasure. But a fact is not an inert substance. It may be modified by new evidence, and it will be subject to new interpretation as contexts shift. If I offer the statistic that from 2016 to 2018 the number of Americans with no healthcare insurance rose by four million,[2] it becomes my responsibility not only to draw inferences from that fact but to give it social and statistical context: Who were those four million? How did the census numbers change in that time? What populations account for that increase? And so on. It is also true that the numbers keep changing. So we track trends, we check back, because facts slip and bump against neighboring facts and change shape.

Once you have a fairly reliable fact, though, and have checked it for accuracy and currency, and checked its source for credibility, there are things you can do with it. You can ask, "If that's true, what else is likely to be true?" Or, "If that's true, what questions does it raise?" Or, "If that's true, what is an appropriate response?" Those three questions open wide doors of reflection and conversation. If it is a fact that in two years the number of unhoused people in my home county grew from 2,822 to 3,665, I have to wonder not only what forces are at work that account for the increase but also what I'm responsible for doing with that information. If I'm willing to know, I need to be willing to act on what I know. I can contribute to fundraisers. I can make sure my church is doing timely blanket and sock drives and helping provide food and temporary shelter. I can inform myself further about where homeless people tend to gather and what their most acute needs are, and I can talk with them. That last may be one of the most significant responses: moving from statistics to a particular street corner is where facts become real.

## Find Facts and Check Them

Specificity is a gift. *This* person on *this* street corner has a story and a constellation of needs and underutilized skills and connections and losses. To know some of those is to witness that one person's life in a more adequate, compassionate, effective way. I think about the way good teachers help young children learn to contextualize others' behavior by reconstructing the facts: "I believe Johnny hit you, but tell me what happened before that. What did you do? Who was watching? Did you do anything to make him feel ashamed or afraid?" And so on. Facts are always linked, but linking them into a narrative is not simple, since multiple narrative strands can be foregrounded and made into the story. There's never just one story to tell; there are many.

One of my favorite exercises in courses on autobiography and memoir is to have students tell their own story, briefly, in these three ways: (1) as a story about loss; (2) as a story about discoveries or achievements; (3) as a story about grace. Each story may be factually accurate, but from each a differently shaded portrait emerges. The exercise can make us a little more aware of how we tell our own stories. It gives an opportunity to reframe those stories and perhaps escape from debilitating versions. One friend to whom I explained the exercise replied, after a long pause, "I think I've been telling my story for years as a story about loss. I've never imagined telling it as a story about grace." In a case like hers, reorganizing the facts of her life—and perhaps exhuming neglected facts—might be profoundly healing.

We expect historians to deal in facts, yet most of us know that those facts can be, and perhaps inevitably are, rearranged according to someone's notion of what matters. I remember my puzzlement when, in college, I read an excerpt from the Anglo-Saxon Chronicle, the earliest record we have of events relating to what is now Great Britain, which spans the centuries from the earliest years of the Christian era to about 1200. Its value as a chronological record is evident, but at times I found myself laughing at what seemed a comically inadequate rendering of "what happened." Many years, of course, were omitted altogether. Many others had only single entries: "48: In this year there was a very severe famine"; "379: This year Gratian succeeded to the empire"; "671: This year was the great destruction among the birds." How can we not want to know what happened to those birds, and why? And who thought that was the single most important thing to remember about the year 671? Yet, as I read, I also found something powerful and compelling about the long list of facts now considered one of the great treasures of English literature and history. They invite us to imagine, connect, invent, infer, speculate, make assumptions and analogies, and consider possibilities. None of those are idle occupations. Those facts are a latticework to which intersecting vines of story may cling and flourish.

My husband had a similar experience in a seminary course on Christian history. Much to his initial disgruntlement, students were required to memorize six pages of single-spaced dates and facts. "Facts are not history," he objected when he brought the list home. And indeed, they are not. And it's hard not to ask yourself at a certain hour of the night who will ever care whether you know what year Martin Luther died or when Constantine called the First Council of Nicaea. And yet, the more time we spend with those facts, the more implications accrue around them, and the more we are able to see them as pivot points in the development of cultural institutions, tensions, movements, or myths. If they had not happened when they did, much else would not have happened. Somehow it continues to matter to me to know that Dante died in 1321 and that Thomas More was beheaded in 1535, and his onetime friend who condemned him to that death, Henry VIII, did not die until 1547. I find myself wondering what those twelve years were like for the king who killed his once dear friend. I find myself considering what else happened in those years and imagining events, like particles, colliding with one another in complex networks of cause and effect.

Causality—even, it turns out, in physics, if you look closely enough—is deceptive. We're never entirely sure what one fact has to do with another, though some lines of causality can be traced easily enough. I was led to muse on this problem with some measure of frustration as a senior in high school when my brother and I took the same course in Western history, taught by a lively, wild storyteller who could take any set of facts and thread them into unforgettable tales. One of his exams consisted of a single question: "Give the causes, major events, and effects of the French Revolution." I wrote for four hours. My brother produced three lists that took him forty-five minutes. We got the same grade. I can only presume that the *A* I felt I richly deserved was for elaboration. His was for concision and clarity.

How we handle the facts we find is always an ethical and social matter. Here, too, a simple repertoire of discernment questions can help us curate the facts at our disposal until we need them to give shape and substance to arguments that need to be made. I was gratified to be able to tell a thoughtful thirteen-year-old why I preferred not to take him to a particular fast-food chain: I gave him a couple of facts about how they treated their workers behind the counter and in slaughterhouses. He listened, and he decided he didn't want to give them his money. He hasn't eaten there since. Last time I checked, though the numbers had changed a bit, conditions had not significantly improved. We still buy our snacks elsewhere.

Facts equip us for compassionate action. They fortify us and give us direction. If we want to do good in the world, they help us imagine where and how that might be possible. And they lead us into story—our stories and others—permitted to fictionalize, but only to a point. They anchor our inferences and keep our imaginations accountable.

Inferences are the stuff of stories—news stories of the kind we hope for as we scroll through much that hardly meets that standard. Sometimes they also lend themselves to fiction—the dystopian fiction that fills shelves and screens and imaginations, perhaps providing a catharsis for the fears we live with, or fiction about ordinary lives lived against a backdrop of uncertainties that calls our attention to the urgency of what we have always known— that we stand in need of prayer, grace, moral courage, awareness, and salvation from the wages of sins that need to be named and resisted by each of us and all of us.

Here are a few helpful examples of people and organizations that seek to uphold high standards of factuality and remind us repeatedly of what magnificent architecture can rise and stand where there is a sound foundation in facts.

## National Geographic

It was my privilege at one time to learn from a writer for this venerable publication. At the time, they employed a roomful of fact-checkers whose business it was to nitpick. The objective was for them to cross-check every single fact or claim in a story for credibility, accuracy, currency, applicability, and relevance. They set a bar so high that even my scrupulous friend found it frustrating at times, though he knew that once his piece went through it would, at least in terms of the facts it presented, be nearly unimpeachable. The magazine retains its reputation for science-based, well-authenticated information and a level of scrupulous care with facts that we need and hope to count on in all reputable periodicals.

## Snopes.com

In their disclosure of methodology, the directors of this fact-checking site remind readers that "since the material we tackle can range from everything to analyzing whether an image has been digitally manipulated to explicating the text of a Congressional bill we can't describe any single method that applies to all of our fact-checking." Included among those methods are contacting living, knowledgeable people who are experts on the topic at hand; going through a representative range of printed material; handing off all research to at least one second editor for a second look; making efforts to use non-partisan, peer-reviewed sources; and providing prompt publication of corrections or clarifications, often from expert readers who bring new sources to light. They also evaluate claims in terms of specific wording, paying attention to the popular usage and possible misperceptions of loaded words. Much of their work is focused on "urban legends" and on claims by persons holding political office or representing officeholders.

My sense of their usability also rests in part on their accessible, human language. We are reminded as we read their analyses that there are real people at real desks peering at real documents in real time, trying to perform a much-needed public service. Their own language matters; they don't retreat to a safe academic distance or pretend to total objectivity, but disclose their own processes as part of a commitment to transparency.

## Politifact

Described on their site and elsewhere as a nonpartisan fact-checking website, Politifact employs a team of researchers and journalists to determine the truth of public claims by political figures, heads of corporations, and other public persons whose representations are subject to the pressures of money and influence. They maintain transparency about all contributions and hold to a stated policy that no contributor has a right to participate in Politifact's truth ratings or assessments of accuracy. The site is run by editors and journalists who cross-check each other's fact-checks, and it is owned by the Poynter Institute for Media Studies.

## Factcheck.org

Like Politifact, this site's stated commitment is to nonpartisan fact-checking of speeches, ads, talk shows, C-SPAN, and other information outlets. It is a project of the Annenberg Public Policy Center at the University of Pennsylvania. It is older than Politifact, and one critic says it "lacks the simplicity" of the other organization, but it is consistently listed among the top half dozen fact-checking organizations.

## The Sunlight Foundation

Like the organizations mentioned above, this nonpartisan group is dedicated to "making government and politics more accountable and transparent." They target specific issues such as web integrity, conflicts of interest in government offices, and lobbying in the legislative process at international, federal, state, and local levels.

9

## *Mind Your Metaphors*

Words are weapons, or instruments, or bridges. Words are bricks in an edifice, or packets of energy, or vessels of prayer. Each of those metaphors opens an avenue of reflection on what words do, how we use them, the kind of power they represent.

Some metaphors, of course, have been flattened into cliché: "That baby is a ray of sunshine." "She's a pistol." "He was met with a wall of silence." We use them so often that we forget they're metaphors that emerge from a particular lineage or realm of human experience. We may not think twice when we hear employees of large corporations (often underpaid) called "family," or an organized group of political partisans described as a "machine," or a friend in distress who tells us she's been on an "emotional roller coaster." Metaphors are pervasive and inevitable. Many of them are enlivening: they give us new ways of noticing and considering experiences or behaviors that might not otherwise occur to us.

Commonplace metaphors are distinguishing features of a language and culture, often odd and untranslatable to foreigners. An irrelevancy in German is *Schnee von gestern*—snow from yesterday. In French, if you have *la cafard*—the cockroach—you're depressed or downhearted. And Spanish speakers who aim to fool you don't "pull your leg" but *toman el pelo*—take your hair. Every metaphorical expression makes its own distinctive appeal to the imagination, offers its own amusement value or (sometimes) shock value, and each is rooted in attitudes and assumptions that go largely unexamined.

Because they carry attitudes and assumptions, metaphors deserve careful examination; their power is something to use with wisdom and good aim. Examining the logic of a metaphor can remind us, sometimes surprisingly, of what we buy into when we use it. One obvious example is metaphors for the body or bodily functions that lead us to think of the body as a machine. A friend who had had four bypass surgeries used to wave away others' concern by insisting, "It's just plumbing." He knew better, but he clearly took some comfort in this reductionistic image of his arteries. He wasn't alone. Lynn Payer, in *Medicine and Culture*, presents evidence for a strong surgical bias in American medicine, which, despite growing respect for more complex, holistic language about the body-mind-energy system, tends still to explain interventions in terms that suggest that organs are simply discrete, replaceable parts. The complex hormonal, neurological, or psychological effects of surgical removals and replacements are still often underemphasized or inadequately understood by hopeful patients who simply want their doctor to do what their car mechanic does: fix the problem—remove the faulty part, dislodge the obstacle, clean out the gunk—and get us back on the road. What tends to be elided in conversations about surgery is the delicate weave of interdependent systems, the complex interactivity of functions we have learned to perceive as distinguishable and therefore separable. We know the body is not a machine, but mechanistic metaphors persist and, according to one recent article, are "getting in the way of scientific progress."[1]

On the other hand, American medical educators are gradually changing the conversation. Organizations such as the American Society for Bioethics and Humanities and a number of standard medical journals such as the *Journal of the American Medical Association*, *Academic Medicine*, and the *American Journal of Bioethics* have recognized, as one editor of the *British Medical Journal* put it:

> Arguably metaphors don't merely describe similarities; they create them. As well as illuminating they can also conceal. It can be hard to think of cancer in a way that is not biomilitary, but wars honour battles which can make the transition to hospice care problematic. Mechanical metaphors for heart disease are also limited as they hold no place for lifestyle modification. . . . I don't actually believe that it would be possible to talk about disease without metaphors. But they have a hidden power that should be understood.[2]

These observations introduce a lively examination of the long-term effects of military metaphors in medicine. Doctors "wage war" on diseases such as cancer. They "bombard" targeted sites with antibiotics or laser treatments. They "attack" and "kill off" and "defeat" viruses and defective cells and encourage patients to think of themselves as "fighters." That these metaphors can be counterproductive has become increasingly apparent, despite the fact that medicine operates in the shadow of the pharmaceutical industry, which intersects uncomfortably with weapons research (early chemotherapies employed active substances that had been developed for chemical warfare). Over the past decade, more and more doctors have begun questioning the conflation of medicine with warfare in clinical discourse; they speak about illness and recovery as a "journey" rather than a "battle." They speak of themselves as "partnering" with patients rather than giving them orders. Some adopt the French idea of the body as terrain and of medical intervention as a process more like amending the soil than attacking. And they are reclaiming medicine not just as a scientific enterprise but also as a healing art, committed to taking both doctor's and patient's subjectivity, sociocultural context, and intuitive moments into account.

Only slightly removed from the military metaphors are those borrowed from sports—a race for the cure, for instance, or the matter of who's on your team. Vyjeyanthi Periyakoil, MD, succinctly observes, in a piece she wrote for the *Journal of Palliative Medicine*,

Sports metaphors invoke all the sports-related axioms and polarize outcomes as a win or lose. They also perpetuate the myth that the patient and the illness are playing on opposing teams and that the illness plays by the rule book. In order to be a true sportsman, the patient has to play it out until the end as "quitting the game" is associated with loss of face.[3]

While marginally less violent than the war metaphors, sports metaphors can tend to trivialize the deeply personal, often spiritual, work of healing, and to entrap the patient in a preconceived "game plan."

Education also suffers from creeping effects of unfortunate metaphors even as educators strive to change the public conversation that shapes their work lives and influences those who fund essential grants and distribute government resources. Language from the world of business and commerce has become commonplace in conversations about education. As an educator, I have been disturbed to hear educators and administrators refer to a school's ability to "deliver" a "product" to students who pay premium prices for tuition and, I have occasionally discovered, indignantly expect to receive the high grade they paid for. Administrators develop "assessment instruments" for collecting "usable data" so as to ensure more consistent "learning outcomes," more effective pricing, and increased competitiveness in the "market." The language of "inputs" and "outcomes" or even "outputs" likens schools to factories and students to raw material waiting to be shaped by a process like manufacture. Even the notion that education is something you "acquire" overlooks the mysterious role of intuition (literally being taught from within) or the subtle effects of ongoing, nuanced conversation that shapes the flow of thought like alluvial pressure.

Thoughtful educators push back. A friend and colleague of mine lightened and sharpened his arguments against destructive metaphors that reduce education to a matter of measurable outcomes by pushing the analogies to a logical extreme in an open letter to the faculty:

> A classroom is not a vending machine in which one deposits a nickel of tuition and receives in return a shiny learning outcome, and learning is not a paint-by-number process. I'm convinced our students learn well when they meet us (and we meet them) in our individual weakness and strangeness, our one-of-a-kind crankiness and quirkiness. The so-called culture of evidence is, I believe, a culture of mistrust and suspicion. It is a culture of homogeneity. It shuns the authentic, the particular, the spontaneous, and enforces adherence to nearly meaningless abstractions.
>
> ... We should ... recall that in a liberal arts college, if a thing is measurable, codifiable, and outcome-labelable, it is probably not worth teaching.[4]

He ended his argument with an invitation: "In that spirit, allow me to call us all, not to further craven compliance, but to joyful, creative resistance." Not only does the "vending machine" suggest how common assessment practices tend toward the mechanical and the simplistic; a final invitation to insurrection reframes resistance as something joyful and creative, life-giving and adventurous, an effort undertaken to preserve what lies at the heart of the work good educators do.

Churches and other religious institutions are also not immune to manipulation by metaphor. The language of business, along with the assumption of a corporate structure and modus operandi, creeps into stewardship campaigns in which fiscal responsibility is measured in familiar terms of maximizing value and efficacy of programs. Evangelism and mission outreach often look unsettlingly like ad campaigns. Few are quite as explicit about this trend as George Barna, who wrote, unabashedly, in his 1988 book, *Marketing the Church*,

> It is time for the church to adopt a whole new paradigm for understanding itself, a model borrowed from the contemporary business world. Like it or not, the church is not only in a market but is itself a business. It has a product to sell, relationship to Jesus and other; its core product is the message of salvation, and each local church is a franchise. The church's pastors will be judged not by their teaching and counseling but their ability to run the church smoothly and efficiently as if it were a business. And like any secular

business, the church must show a profit, which is to say it must achieve success in penetrating and servicing its market.[5]

While I would like to think that the confusion of mission with marketing has come under more critical scrutiny in the ensuing decades, a recent article by Tim Schraeder similarly adopts the corporate model and metaphor without much critical scrutiny. In it he offers "4 Must-Know Church Marketing Secrets."[6] But marketing is not the same as an invitation to approach the table, contemplate mysteries, listen for divine guidance, enter into mystical community, or learn from those who have experienced spiritual awakening. It is not even the same as thoughtful argument or religious education. Marketing lures. Ministry invites and welcomes.

The effects of deeply embedded metaphors are not only conceptual; every metaphor suggests an approach or strategy. Medical interventions, the design of entrance exams, recruitment of young people into the military, acceptance of hierarchy and institutional authority all rest in part on metaphors that normalize some behaviors and suppress others.

As a culture, we have normalized increased violence with our ubiquitous war metaphors—not only in medicine—and have come to tolerate a loss of civilian life, environmental destruction, and endless conflict, profitable to a privileged minority at the cost of many others' lives. War is one of our most widespread, all-purpose metaphors—unsurprising in a nation that spends over 60 percent of its budget on the military. In my lifetime we have seen "wars" on poverty, on drugs, on crime, on cancer, on terrorism. We've been involved in "trade wars" and "culture wars" and "wars of ideas." Political statements about the "war on Christmas" or the "war on women" or the "war on cops" or the "war on science" invoke the metaphor to make issues or causes more visible and urgent, though by now, simply by dint of overuse, I would guess it has become somewhat less effective than it once was. But calling an intellectual or philosophical disagreement a war, or calling a change in the ways we seek to prevent crimes a war, or calling an effort to solve the problem of poverty a war—all of these mask and oversimplify the hard work of analysis, deliberation, and negotiation by an appeal to emotional zeal.

I've named several large areas of public concern in which the conversation is shaped and directed by metaphors, but just as pertinent to most of us, most of the time, is the way we invoke metaphors in ordinary, daily conversations. A good metaphor adds spice or spark or sharpens the point or softens the blow . . . choose your metaphor! I have a friend, a financial advisor, whose particular gift lies in finding unusual metaphors for explaining to clients less versed in the language of finance how hedge funds or mutual funds or IRAs work. When he talks about risk, he speaks about how many steps we want to take into the water before we might begin to lose our footing. He talks about how to get better "gas mileage" from investments. He punctuates conversation about aging and actuarial tables with football analogies, pointing out that we're "past the fifty-yard line." He's a person of faith. He knows life on this earth is temporary, and all metaphors point to realities beyond practical immediacies. His metaphors are an education in themselves. They not only help me understand; they get me beyond the creeping boredom I admit to feeling whenever the subject of financial management can no longer be avoided.

I know people who knit or sew who naturally speak of connection in terms of stitching, binding, and seams. People who love to cook might well report that a speaker was delicious to listen to, or that the music at an evening event was depressingly bland. Because I have spent so much of my life teaching literature, it's not surprising to me how often I speak of events in terms of plot twists or denouements or comic relief, or of life's troubles as "part of the assignment" or something that must have been "in the lesson plan." We reach for what we know well to find our way into what is unfamiliar and sometimes unsettling. Metaphors help us domesticate what is slightly bewildering.

And they help us laugh. I still chuckle over a story Anne Lamott told in a public talk about her son, who, when he realized he was finally taller than she, put his arms around her and said, "You are a little gnome to me." Somehow I still find myself giggling when someone describes listening to a lecture packed with information as trying to "drink from a firehose." It always made me smile when a colleague would begin a conversation at the end of a day of teaching and office hours with the query, "How are your patients?," and when another colleague would conclude his critiques of administrators with some comment about what he would do if he "ran the zoo." Occasionally he reverted to the adage about herding cats. I've watched cats. I'm one of the cats. I'm fine with that.

While we're on the subject of minding our metaphors, here are five that deserve particular consideration.

## Body

> **body** (body of Christ, body politic, body of the message, body of work, the gathered body of congressional voters)

The metaphor of the body always serves as a reminder of unity, diversity within unity, complexity, and the dynamic character of the systems we inhabit. Even a brief exposure to the study of anatomy must take us beyond simplistic, mechanistic notions of the digestive system as plumbing or the nervous system as electrical wiring: we are not machines, but mysterious, incarnate beings, "fearfully and wonderfully made" (Ps. 139:14). Paul's introduction of the term "body of Christ" in Romans 12:5 ("so we, who are many, are one body in Christ, and individually we are members one of another") is, if we take it seriously, a shocking and radical understanding of the mystical bond that unites us more intimately than blood relationship; certainly it goes beyond notions of common assent to dogma or shared sensibilities or mutual vested interests. If you push the metaphor to its contemporary limits, considering the interplay of endocrine and hormonal systems, new discoveries about how "brain" functions are distributed throughout the body, and what goes on at the cellular and molecular levels, there is a lifetime of learning to do about what it means to be members of one another and of one body. Look around. That's who we are together—vulnerable, powerful, trainable, subject to environmental contamination, susceptible to placebos, in need of healing, and capable of rejuvenation and ultimately transformation.

The implications of the metaphor in "body politic" are much more limited, but also consequential. The term has a slightly antique ring now; it originated in the Middle Ages, and it has had a long lineage of serious real-world effects, beginning with the idea of the sovereign as "head" of the state, even though some sovereigns have defied any commonsense understanding of how a "head" functions. Every major part of the body has been appropriated as metaphor in this context: an "arm" of government; who "has a hand" in decision-making; who serves as official "mouthpiece"; who publishes "digests" of parliamentary or congressional proceedings; whether a piece of legislation has "teeth"; and so on. The deception implicit in the metaphor is that a system of governance designed by human beings for (some) human purposes is somehow a natural, organic entity. Historian Garry Wills has written extensively of the way Lincoln appropriated this idea in the Gettysburg Address in his efforts to reunite a fractured nation: the language of a nation "conceived" in liberty, being "brought forth" by our "fathers," substitutes the idea of "birth of a nation" for the historical fact of a system created on sweaty afternoons in Philadelphia by a contentious group of white, male, propertied (some slave-owning) politicians who managed to arrive at an intelligent compromise that promised to serve most of their economic purposes. We can ill afford to forget the difference; no system of governance is sacred in the way a human being is sacred, or mysterious in the way the human body-mind-spirit is mysterious and beyond our making.

The word "corporation," of course, extends the body metaphor perhaps more dangerously to entities that are anything but natural or organic, but are created for the profit of a specified group of private investors. Benevolent as their beginnings may have been, some corporations have become behemoths that control more assets than governments and have proven themselves capable of holding whole nations hostage to their interests. (See, for instance, the 2009 documentary *Crude*, which tracks the activity of Chevron in Ecuador, or any of several documentaries about the effects of the Monsanto Corporation on small farmers in India and around the world.)

We extend the body metaphor in many other ways, some of which are suggested above. To speak of a writer's or artist's body of work is to see the totality of what they have produced as one more or less unified, evolving whole. This has some critical merit; it enables us to trace the trajectory of intellectual and artistic development as we might the growth of a child to an adult and into the gradual losses of age. We speak of the will of the body with reference to loose gatherings of interested parties at city council or faculty or parent meetings. All of these uses help us see the parts within the frame of a whole. All of them deserve to be used with care.

**Wave**

> **wave** (of nausea, pain, heat, political action or reaction)

Many of us who have gone through childbirth training have learned to "ride the waves" of painful contractions. It is not uncommon in other medical settings to speak of a similar skill of riding waves of nausea, pain, fear, anxiety, or vertigo. The implication is a hopeful one: waves crest and break and recede. Even the giant Hawaiian waves we see in surfing movies, though they may be life-threatening, are generally survivable. One way to survive them is to dive directly into them. Waves cannot be stopped, but their force can be evaded by what may seem the counterintuitive move of entering them rather than trying to flee.

Like the body metaphor, the image of the wave is natural: waves and tides are controlled by the pull of the moon—a force far beyond human control. When we learn about the relation of tides to lunar cycles we are reminded of the smallness of the planet and of its "membership" in a larger system that is part of an even larger system contained in yet larger systems that have to be described in terms of light-years and powers of ten. Because they can be survived but not stopped, waves pose a threat different from attacks. And they are not only threatening but beautiful, graceful, and sometimes gentle. There is hope in the image of a wave.

Living in an area where heat waves are recurrent and often dangerous, we are trained to expect and hope that the heat will abate over time, so we find air conditioning or shade or a pond or a pool and wait it out. In this era of climate change, however, that optimistic metaphor may not be as applicable as heretofore.

Similarly, the notion of a wave of political activism, as in references to the "third wave" of feminism, may usefully describe movements in terms of recurrence, gradual accumulation of energy, gathered force, breaking points, and periods of ebbing, but it doesn't take into account the kinds of lasting structural and conceptual changes that are hoped for and sometimes brought about by people who meet, make agreements, and push established processes to new purposes.

## Building

**building** (architectural/structural metaphors vs. natural metaphors)

We build consensus, or lay the foundations for a new organizational vision, or buttress our ideas with new data. We realize the goal will have to be accomplished brick by brick. We take care to nail down prescribed procedures. We get rid of old wood and hope to open doors or at least windows that can help circulate new ideas like fresh air through old institutions. Faulkner was not the only writer to describe his work in terms of "joining" or carpentry or building; architectural metaphors for written work emphasize structure, stability, and resistance to forces that might threaten what is being protected and sometimes hidden within.

Sometimes the metaphor of building focuses on that stability and protection at the expense of a more dynamic vision of how ideas or organizations live and move and have their being. It backgrounds ideas like fluidity or resilience or adaptability. Especially in language-related endeavors, if we construct an argument on the basis of notions of strength and sturdiness against attack, we might miss the pliancy of ambiguity; we may fail to take into account the value of compromise and the fact that the terms in which one frames the argument may change, the conditions in which it applies may change, or (gasp!) our minds may change when new evidence comes to light.

## Bears and Hens

**bears** and **hens** (metaphors for the good mother)

I have on occasion heard women who are particularly active, protective advocates for their children—sometimes children with special needs they feel are not being acknowledged by schools—described as "mama bears." I've also heard the term applied to women who are particularly physically affectionate with their children, and who seem to derive some of their own energy from intimate, physical engagement with children. Sometimes "mama bear" types turn aggressive toward those who seem to threaten their children. Researchers have reported that 70 percent of human deaths caused by grizzly bears come from mothers protecting their young.[7] The metaphor is two-sided, at least, though actually much more multifaceted.

The metaphor of the mother hen goes back to biblical times and beyond—most memorably, perhaps, when Jesus laments over the wayward people he loves: "O Jerusalem, Jerusalem, . . . how often would I have gathered your children together as a hen gathers her brood under her wings" (Matt. 23:37 RSV). People who raise hens witness the way a mother hen will put herself at risk, cackling, rushing headlong, and pushing her chicks behind her wings to protect them from a dog or predator. On the nest, mother hens will turn their eggs up to thirty times a day to maintain proper temperature, moisture, and ventilation and will make soothing sounds the chicks apparently register. She stays calm while they peck their tentative way out of their shells. There's a lot to admire in the hen, and a lot of positive encouragement in the metaphor to recognize and reinforce mothers' instinctual courage and often self-sacrificial strategies for protecting their young, though often when women are described as "mother hens" what is alluded to is a tendency toward anxious overprotectiveness, often beyond the age when it's appropriate, and possibly impeding a child's progress toward healthy independence.

Both of these metaphors, and others that link human mothers to animal mothers (Mother Goose, for instance, though the origins of that name are contested and complicated), while they suggest and encourage behaviors our culture has come to associate with "good" mothering, also perpetuate a strong link between mothering behavior and animal instinct, downplaying the role of rational decision-making, negotiation with partners, economic pressures, accessibility to extended family or community, faith communities, social services, and nutritional food sources in child raising—to name just a few of the many factors involved in raising children now. So the danger of the metaphor lies, as is so often the case, in the ways it can, carelessly used, oversimplify, relegate, and stereotype.

**Dirt**

**dirt** (smut vs. healthy notion of soil)

One of my favorite books among many fine ones by contemporary science writers is *Dirt* by William Bryant Logan. The subtitle is *The Ecstatic Skin of the Earth*. It is a beautifully detailed, thoughtful, poetic explanation of and reflection on how soil on this earth came from stardust, what elements healthy soil requires to produce healthy food, and how soil is replenished or dies. The title plays deliberately at the edges of the commonplace metaphor: we think easily of who has the "dirt" on a hushed-up story, of "dirty" novels or films, of "dirty" language, and of dirt as filth. But "dirt" and "filth" are not synonymous. The danger of dismissing dirt as something unworthy of sustained consideration is that, as one farmer argued, soil depletion may be one of the most pressing crises of our time, though it is one that gets very little publicity and about which there is relatively little public education. Soil can die, he reminded us in a sobering talk several years ago. And when soil dies, it can no longer be used to produce food. Monoculture, the cultivation of a single crop rather than diverse and complementary crops, inhibits the natural replenishment of soil. Much of our agribusiness relies on monoculture for the sake of convenience and efficiency. That we need more awareness of our deep dependence on the life of the soil is a point made in many documentaries about food production. It is a point we would do well to make in schools and places of worship. That we are made from this earth, that we are dust, that for those of us who receive communion the bread and wine are (as some liturgies say) gifts that "earth has given" are truths that bear repeating weekly, daily.

10

## Complicate Matters

My brother, a devoted teacher of math, physics, and astronomy who has also read widely in theology, still gets a laugh out of the joke about the condescending astronomer who asks a theologian, "Doesn't it all really just come down to 'Love your neighbor'?" After a polite pause the theologian replies, "I suppose you could say that—sort of the way astronomy all really comes down to 'Twinkle, twinkle, little star.'" The joke delivers a pertinent message: we face a culture increasingly driven by oversimplified political messages, abbreviations, memes, tweets, and ads that leave little time or room for nuance. Scholars and analysts who do the careful, slow, lapidary work that takes full account of ambiguities, anomalies, irregularities, and indeterminacies compete with glib formulas and overblown images often designed to forestall close inspection.

I have told generations of students in literature courses that the task of the good novelist or nonfiction writer is to complicate. Some of them appear to believe that Herman Melville, Henry James, William Faulkner, and James Joyce took that task rather too much to heart. But their word-weary complaints bring up an interesting question: What were those writers with their twelve-line sentences and oblique references being faithful to? What operations of the mind or intimations of the imagination or currents of history could only be adequately conveyed by means of complicated syntax? I believe—or I wouldn't have spent time teaching their novels—that their aim was to elucidate, not confuse.

Complexity is not the opposite of clarity. Oversimplification is a dangerous tool—deceptive, manipulative, and alluring. As columnist Ellen Goodman once said at the conclusion of a talk about journalism, "The bottom line is always 'It's not that simple.'" To speak with integrity in the public square is to insist on more than the sound bite; to insist that there are more than two sides to an argument; to insist that authentic debate move beyond either/or questions, three-point plans, and slogans. One of the arts we need to cultivate for the common good is the craft of simplifying without dumbing down—making sophisticated ideas accessible without avoiding complexity. Good popularizers are servants of truth and faith and democracy; they make it possible for those of us who haven't had a chance to study physics or Hebrew or medicine to consider the merits of space travel or the ambiguities of Scripture or to weigh the tradeoffs among treatment plans with some basis for opinion and choice. I admire Oliver

Sacks's clinical tales for the window they provide on neurological disorders, Jeremie Begbie's elegant excursions into music theory for those who rely on songs to meet needs and longings, and Eugene Peterson's paraphrase of the Bible for the way it reinvigorates the sacred text for so many. These are all writers who translate for the common reader with deep commitment to honoring the complexities. All three of these writers speak with a hard-won simplicity that can be achieved only by extensive study, reflection, and clarity about what lies at the heart of the complicated matters they address—neuropathologies, the physics of musical vibrations, Hebrew Scripture with all its jots and tittles.

All of us—not just the experts—find ourselves occasionally in the position of having to render difficult, elusive, complicated experiences in a way that makes them accessible to those who haven't gone through anything similar. Studying writing by patients with terminal or chronic illness or disability gave me considerable respect for the way patients who honor the felt nuances of pain, suffering, loss, and hope can keep doctors and medical decision-makers accountable by reminding them not to underestimate the stories they step into. As medicine is increasingly driven by insurance companies' bottom lines, it becomes more urgent for medical practice to be informed by real people's messy, sorrowful, engaging, entangled stories. One of my favorite patient poets, Karen Fiser, for instance, writes these lines about a surgery that left her in great pain and aware that she was beginning a life of chronic pain (they are part of a longer poem):

> I went to sleep as one woman—silken, magic,
>     strong—
> my life full of intelligence, bravura episodes
> and turns of phrase. I woke up all stitching
>     and sorrow,
> with a silence around me like the endless
>     quiet
> at the edges of a late Rembrandt self-portrait.
>
> Time spent in pain exists absolutely, without
>     structure,
> demarcation or relief, it is all one color,
> like winter's rainy *sfumato* inscriptions on
>     gray.
> Meanwhile, the other, inner life goes on,
>     unwitnessed,
> the shadow a tree makes on the wall, rippling
>     like water.[1]

To read these lines is to learn something subtle and challenging about the complexity of pain that no pill can address. The disorientation, the alteration of the sense of self, and the isolation may not be dimensions of pain that medicine can adequately address, but for a doctor to carry into her clinical encounters something of this awareness would be to resist a little harder a medical system that subjects most of those in it to pressures that diminish relationality and hurries us all along to the cure. Good doctors, like good soldiers, dwell in perpetual paradox, acknowledge ambiguities and uncertainties, and take the time to enlarge the fine print.

We have certainly witnessed consequences of oversimplification in news reporting and political debate over the past couple of decades as whole people groups have been labeled and vilified (often without even minimal understanding of the Qur'an or Middle Eastern customs or Arabic); national security has come down to a twenty-one-foot wall; the Bible has been watered down and weaponized; and every supermarket checkout counter features magazines whose cover stories reduce relationships or health or financial management to five or seven easy steps. Navigating the complexities of any of those takes time and reflection, not to mention prayer and attention to subtleties that escape the hurried eye. Inducing citizens and consumers to pay that closer attention—read articles, listen to lectures or TED talks or podcasts, watch documentaries—is challenging in the midst of the "too-muchness" of many American lives.

Seeing more complexly involves widening the lens through which we look. We see poor health—diabetes, for instance, or obesity and heart disease—more complexly if we ask questions not only about what individuals eat but about the food systems they inhabit and the economic and cultural pressures upon them to eat fast food and packaged food with high sugar content, shop in convenience stores, and consume too much alcohol at the end of the day. We see poor student performance in school more complexly if we ask questions that go beyond how a particular student is using her time and consider why so many are being diagnosed with attention deficit disorder, how many come to school poorly nourished, how many are being bullied or harassed, how many just need the few more minutes of personal attention that might be possible if a classroom held twenty rather than forty students. We see poverty differently if we learn how many in this country are only two paychecks away from homelessness, how few families can afford for one parent to be at home, how little margin minimum-wage jobs provide for sick kids or broken cars. We see culture wars differently if we inquire about fears rather than presuming evil motives. We understand faith differently if we stop trying to reduce it to propositions and precepts and allow room for story and mystery to invite us to dwell in uncertainty, experience timelessness, develop hope on new terms.

Even those of us who read and listen carefully can be tempted by simplistic diagnoses of problems or resolutions of them. The main temptation is closure. Closure is comfortable, and comforting, even when it leaves a problem unsolved. Simple equations like "She's an addict because she made bad choices" or "The school is failing because the teachers aren't doing their jobs" or "Their kids are in trouble because they don't discipline them at home" allow us, if we're passing judgment, to rest satisfied that we've at least parsed the problem if not solved it. But the more I see of the damage simplistic thinking can do, the more I admire and cling to John Keats's notion of "negative capability," which he defined as the capacity to dwell in ambiguity or paradox without "any irritable reaching after fact & reason."[2] To allow room for wonder, speculation, uncertainty.

I believe we can develop negative capability, though doing so may require a little help from our friends and the courage to swim upstream. A first step toward becoming more negatively capable is to ask a wider range of questions. One valuable practice is to apply each of the six question words—"who," "what," "when," "where," "how," and "why"—to a situation or behavior before you make a judgment. For instance, who are the influencers? How did this person's situation leave him open to self-defeating choices? What is at stake, and for whom? What pressures—financial, social, or psychological—may be operative? When did this story begin? What was in place before this person even knew there was a decision to be made? Why might someone engage in self-destructive behavior? Each of those questions adds a subplot or sidebar to a story and serves as a reminder that no human story is only about an individual. It is only when we begin to question the "obvious"— that is, to suspect that whatever seems obvious, isn't—that we pause and raise the questions that reframe.

Another practice that I have found helpful when I'm tempted to pass snap judgments or settle for simplistic arguments is to pause. Just pause. Wait before agreeing with a persuasive speaker; pause before offering an opinion; let there be a little silence around the edges of any statement—my own or others'—in which to hear whether it rings true. Pause when something on the page in front of you gives you pause. Then go in before you go on: wonder what it was that stopped you. Follow whatever wisp of feeling or shadow of a question was triggered by some word choice or image or claim. Spend a little time between the lines, behind the words. Tug on the threads that dangle from them. See what comes. What comes is likely to complicate the message and the moment. Welcome complication. Another word for it is richness. Complexity is the mother of surprise.

Before we move on from our reflections on complexity, let us pause for a moment of negative capability: I'd like to leave you with four examples of problematic oversimplifications that need to be called out and complicated, whenever we speak or write about them.

## Pro and Con

I once joked to the provost at the college where I was teaching that, as a complement to the debating tournament the college hosted every year, we should hold "Ambiguity Olympics." Somehow the idea never took root. My point was that debating, though it cultivates impressive skills at marshaling evidence and presenting and defending arguments, is generally organized on the premise that there are two sides to a question: pro and con. Of course, people intelligent enough to be involved in debate are capable of recognizing that on any important question there is a vast and topographically treacherous middle ground, but the structure of debate as we learn it in school, and as we play it out in the two-party system, tends to thrust us into either/or choices that don't allow much room for creative compromise.

Those of us who watch courtroom dramas or congressional hearings or occasionally witness real court proceedings are familiar with the two-edged effect of a lawyer's insistence that a witness "answer yes or no." Sometimes it is a way of cutting through evasive language. Sometimes, on the other hand, it is a way of forestalling important explanation, qualification, modification, or contextualizing that might help to acknowledge the ambiguities and complexities of the situation at hand. In that case, insisting on yes or no, pro or con is, itself, a dangerous evasion.

## Race

Much has been written about the ways in which this term—not to mention the social and political realities for which it has become shorthand—has a costly, shameful, and complicated history. A 2016 article in *Scientific American* argues, based on a good bit of academic research, that "race" is a social construct, and racial categories are "a weak proxy for genetic diversity" that should be "phased out."[3] Geneticists find it too crude to provide useful information. Genetic variations among people groups don't reveal a single "absolute genetic difference" or variant that distinguishes one group—say, Africans—from another—say, Europeans. The suggestion that somehow "race" is a biological category has done incalculable harm, beginning with the ways it has lent support to theories of biological superiority of one people group over another, and continuing in the ways it is factored into conversations about poverty or crime or social pathologies as though a meaningful causal connection could be found.

Even efforts to dispel "racial" inequality or bias can sometimes backfire insofar as they perpetuate the category. Even as we are legally bound not to discriminate on the basis of "race, class, religion, or gender," we continue to internalize the idea that race is a category like those others, while it operates on a very different history and set of assumptions.

"Race" is often conflated with "ethnicity"; though the terms are distinguishable, often the distinctions given in popular sources are misleading, the former being presumed or perceived to refer to biological characteristics, and the latter to cultural differentia. It may be that we need to do what we can to retire the word "race" and speak, when it's relevant, only in terms of "ethnicity," acknowledging the many variables that term includes. In any case, the word "race" remains a volatile and dangerous oversimplification, always worth qualifying and tempering as we go.

## Reading

Reading is a prerequisite for effective participation in cultural and political process in the postindustrial, post-modern world. Though the published literacy rate for the United States is still over 90 percent, that number reflects only minimal competence. Reading well—reading discerningly, critically; contextualizing appropriately; understanding implications; making distinctions between what is literal and what is figurative; asking questions about sources and bias—is far less common. Even the competent readers I have worked with in college classrooms generally have a long way to go before they can read with the kind of discriminating eye and critical tools required to interpret difficult, ambiguous, antique, or specialized texts appropriately. That's why we continue to teach reading at the college level; more remains to be learned about how language works. One online discussion of literacy rates reminds us, "literacy skills are complex and span . . . a range of proficiency shades, while literacy rates assume a sharp, binary distinction between those who are and those who aren't 'literate.'"[4]

Semi-literacy is arguably more dangerous than illiteracy. Simplistic readings of important texts have led to violence: consider what happens, for instance, when the Bible or the Constitution is read selectively, out of historical context, in order to promote a singular political agenda. Far too many wars have been fought over competing readings of the Bible. Variant readings of passages in the Constitution bring constitutional lawyers into vociferous public debate.

So when someone crisply announces that they've read the four Gospels and know what they say, or have read *Moby-Dick* and find it boring, I wonder what they mean by "read." It takes more than one reading—sometimes many— to glean all that some texts offer. Even then, the richest texts support more than one reading. One can read *King Lear* as a play about power, or as a play about honesty, or as a play about love. It is all of those, but depending on which thread one pulls on, it is possible to arrive at very different readings of the play.

Reading involves looking and looking again. It involves consent to the writer's terms but also, occasionally, resistance to those terms. It involves suspension of disbelief, critical scrutiny, empathy, imagination, forgiveness, self-awareness, openness, judgment. Even what is inscribed in stone is subject to the shifting light of the human gaze.

## Family

In North American middle-class culture, the term "family" is, I believe, most often understood to refer to the nuclear family, though historically the extended family—mixed, messy, and shifting—has been more the norm. The so-called traditional family—one father, one mother, married and living together with their biological children—is shrinking statistically, giving way to a range of nontraditional families. Even in the most conventional family structures, the question of who is "family" arises on ritual occasions when one wonders how far out on the kinship diagram to extend the invitation list. And many groups of people who think of one another as "family" are circles of people unrelated by blood who have chosen to live together, perhaps care for children, sharing resources and time and stories.

The term "family" has been confused by metaphorical expropriation: corporations frequently use it to describe employees, creating a false sense of belonging and trust that is deceptive in the way it masks the essentially economic nature of the relationship between employers and workers.

Jesus complicated our understanding of family on several occasions—a matter worth raising with those who regard any but the nuclear family of blood kin as outsiders. In Matthew 12:47–49, for instance, he replies to a messenger sent from his mother to summon him, "Who is my mother, and who are my brothers?" And stretching out his hand toward his disciples, he said, "Here are my mother and my brothers!"

Protection of families, care for family life, and nurturing children in healthy families are unquestionably important. Defining family generously, flexibly, in real-life contexts, recognizing how people are drawn into lasting commitments and the love that keeps them there, this matters now, as we look around us and see families falling apart and families reconstructing themselves out of the "heap of broken images."[5]

11

## *Laugh When You Can*

A host of politically engaged comedians over the past couple of decades have proven how effectively comedy can expose hidden agendas and unsettle the complacent. In 2015 a survey reported in *The Atlantic* suggested that over 10 percent of "millennials" trusted their favorite political comedians more than they trusted most network news outlets. Among Christians, a refreshing voice came for years from Brian Doyle, a writer of poems and pithy essays who included in his *Book of Uncommon Prayer* a "Prayer for Osama bin Laden, Yes Even Him the Stupid Murderous Slime," which begins, "Because if I cannot pray grudgingly ragingly reluctantly furiously confusedly complicatedly for *his* shattered soul, what is the point of praying at all?"[1] Doyle modeled for many of us a rich, theologically informed faith that included the firm conviction that, living by grace, we can afford to laugh.

We can afford to laugh if we are deeply convinced that the love of God is "broader than the measures of the mind,"[2] that we don't have to trudge uphill to meet a grim

and punitive God, that laughter is not the opposite of se-
riousness, but often a characteristic of capacious minds
capable of complexity, ambiguity, and appreciation of
mystery. People who lace their conversation, even about
important things, with real humor remind us all that there
is room for grace.

I say "real" humor because of course we see on every
network and social media outlet examples of glib, cheap
humor that goes for quick laughs by appealing to prurience
or pettiness or prejudice. But real humor, characterized by
intelligent wit, sudden reframing, open-heartedness, and
loving solidarity, lightens and enlightens the conversations
we live by. Some of it is wry: some truths are most effectively
told by means of irony. Some of it is boisterous. Some of it is
subtle as a sidelong smile. I think, for instance, of surprising
moments in T. S. Eliot's ceremonial and deeply serious *Four
Quartets*—poems that lift us into mystical realms of con-
templation and reflection on spiritual experience—which
drop us suddenly into the ordinary with an occasional gentle thump, as when he writes about

> The moments of happiness—not the sense of
>   well-being,
> Fruition, fulfillment, security or affection,
> Or even a very good dinner ...[3]

The "very good dinner" suddenly introduces into a series of lofty abstractions a mundane particularity of daily

life that is also, rightly, an important part of the happiness we are to hope for. Like the "daily bread" in the Lord's Prayer, such reminders insist that we acknowledge that, as another poet put it, "I am here in body, / a passenger, and rumpled."[4] Writers or speakers whose message sticks usually find ways to surprise us into laughter, or at least a flicker of amusement at our own pretensions.

As we consider how to minister by words, it's good to hold onto the simple truth that amusement matters. The expression "deadly serious" ought to tell us something: beyond a point, serious can be deadly. Laughter is leaven. Laughter loosens what is cramped or clutched. It opens our breathing and releases tension. We laugh when we're relieved. We laugh when we're genuinely surprised. We laugh when children make oddly accurate observations, when puppies crawl and squirm over each other for food, when family members allude to shared moments of comic failure. We laugh over incongruous word choices, sudden shifts of tone, metaphors that stretch meaning. We laugh out of sympathy or expectation or rueful self-recognition. I'd like here to explore a few kinds of laughter we need to cultivate and encourage to keep our discourse life-giving.

One is *corrective laughter*—the kind that says, "You must be kidding." Laughing at what deserves—and urgently needs—to be recognized as truly ridiculous is a healthy exercise of faith and democracy. It may come as a refusal to accept absurdly biased or self-interested policy

proposals, or as a rejection of identifiable lies or deceptions. It unmasks. In his article "Humor as a Social Corrective," Avner Ziv observes, "Writers of comedy are well
aware that the subjects with which they deal—infidelity,
self-importance, hypochondria, and all the rest—will continue to exist. What comedy really does is to place them beneath a magnifying glass."[5] Seeing them for what they are,
and laughing, we return to the shared ground of common
sense. Some things deserve to be laughed out of court, or
out of serious consideration. In restoring common sense,
we restore a sense of the commons—what we hold in common, the common ground we share as humans making our
journeys together on "this fragile earth, our island home."
We call one another back from isolation, inflation, excess,
insularity. To speak the word that sparks a laugh is, in a
sense, a priestly function.

Then there is *restorative laughter*—the kind that says,
"It's all okay. Let's begin again." It insists that there is life
beyond brokenness and betrayal, beyond disappointment
and defeat, that heavy things can be made light, that all
can—and will—in the longest run be well. Restorative
laughter allays anxieties by offering a new angle of vision.
Moments of laughter at twelve-step meetings where personal stories of considerable pain are shared are often of
this kind, or the laughter that comes in the midst of ten-
sion-ridden meetings about intra-departmental disputes
or familial conflict. Occasionally, even on the floor of Congress, laughter erupts on both sides of the aisle, as several

times happened in the bipartisan interview with Mark Zuckerberg about Facebook's use of user data: the stakes were high and the matter serious, but now and then everyone involved was able, for a moment, to step back and "get real" about the fact that we all know certain games are being played, certain evasions are predictable, certain questions are pro forma. To laugh was to acknowledge that there is something about the human comedy that we cannot escape, even in moments of critical confrontation, and that to recognize this is to retain our humanity despite our deep and consequential differences. These moments are precious, indeed. Laughter like this is a gift; it can't be manufactured for the occasion, but should certainly be welcomed when it blows through the room like the breath of the Spirit.

Then there is the *laughter of sheer celebration*. It's been my privilege to be present at a number of births besides those of my own children. Almost always, after the last cry of labor is released and the child is caught and held up and wrapped and put in the mother's arms, there are both tears and laughter. Life has happened again—new and fresh and tiny and messy and squalling. The babies' heads sometimes look funny and they're covered with vernix and their noses wrinkle and their little arms flail. And their every move delights us. We laugh to celebrate and welcome them. We laugh when new graduates wave their diplomas from the stage, and when the newly married couple emerges from the ceremony and we throw confetti or birdseed or flower petals in a show of abundance. The words we say on those occasions are secondary and often conventional, but they weave a space for the laughter, and give it structure, and make it memorable.

"Prepare for mirth," Shakespeare writes, "for mirth becomes a feast." In a sense, all we do to invite and encourage healthy, life-giving, life-affirming laughter is preparation for a feast. The vision of the heavenly banquet, however one imagines or interprets it, is an expression of hope that is foreshadowed by our laughter here, in the long valley where we labor on our way. The richest, purest laughter is holy—a sign of joy that can be induced by words but takes us beyond them. The final paragraph of G. K. Chesterton's *Orthodoxy* leaves us with a radical suggestion that laughter lies at the hidden heart of the gospel message, so often reduced, tragically, in the hands of the unimaginatively earnest, to admonition and warning. Chesterton offers a long backward glance over the gospel stories, inviting us to imagine the life of Jesus in all its mystery and paradox:

> His pathos was natural, almost casual. . . . He never concealed His tears; He showed them plainly on His open face at any daily sight, such as the far sight of His native city. Yet He concealed something. . . . He never restrained His anger. He flung furniture down the front steps of the Temple, and asked men how they expected to escape the damnation of Hell. Yet He restrained something. . . . There was something

that He hid from all men when He went up a mountain to pray. There was something that He covered
constantly by abrupt silence or impetuous isolation.
There was some one thing that was too great for God
to show us when He walked upon our earth; and I
have sometimes fancied that it was His mirth.[6]

If we enter into that "fancy," as we travel back through
those sacred texts, we may indeed find ourselves smiling,
if not laughing, over those moments when Jesus met the
Pharisees' warnings with wit, or when he wondered aloud
at the obtuseness of his bumbling and bewildered disciples, or perhaps when Peter leapt out of the boat, saw what
he was doing, lost his nerve, and began to sink.

U. A. Fanthorpe, another devout writer unafraid to find
and name the comedy in the most sacred of Christian stories, imagines Jesus's rueful frustration at the disciples' very
human foibles—the stuff of which all comedy is made—as
he laments what he has to put up with:

> . . . Pete, with his headband stuffed with
>     fishhooks,
> His gift for rushing in where angels wouldn't,
> Tom, for whom metaphor is anathema,
> And James and John, who want the room at
>     the top—
> These numskulls are my medium. I called
>     them.

I am tattooing God on their makeshift lives.
My Keystone Cops of disciples, always
Running absurdly away, or lying ineptly,
Cutting off ears and falling into the water,
These Sancho Panzas must tread my Quixote
    life,
Dying ridiculous and undignified,
Flayed and stoned and crucified upside down.
They are the dear, the human, the dense, for
    whom
My message is. That might, had I not touched
    them,
Have died decent respectable upright deaths
    in bed.[7]

To join Fanthorpe in her laughter is to be humbled out of creeping sanctimoniousness or too-solemn piety or pretension, and to recognize in godly patience something wonderfully, joyfully generous.

All spiritual traditions, it seems, share this spark of comedy: the piquant tales of the early desert fathers find their counterpart in the bubbling pleasure on the Dalai Lama's face as he bows, often strangely amused, to crowds of Western business managers or devotees clutching notebooks. Native American teaching tales are laced with sometimes bawdy laughter;[8] Taoist Zhuangzi is noted for gently mocking his disciples' pretensions;[9] and Hindu teachers insist that, when we see things as they are, we will laugh at our delusions.[10] We need these reminders from elders and teachers, and from those who have suffered and survived, and from those who have witnessed horror and nevertheless urge us to accept and celebrate the life we get. One of my favorites among such reminders is the image William Butler Yeats offers at the end of his poem "Lapis Lazuli"—a meditation on a small statue of "Two Chinamen, and behind them a third" ascending a mountain. The speaker imagines them, arrived at the top of the mountain, surveying the wide, sad landscape of human history, so full of atrocities and threats, wars and rumors of wars, newly escalated in the new century. They look out upon it all from a distance that enables them to see what we, caught in the thick of our fears and fighting, cannot:

> There, on the mountain and the sky,
> On all the tragic scene they stare.
> One asks for mournful melodies;
> Accomplished fingers begin to play.
> Their eyes mid many wrinkles, their eyes,
> Their ancient, glittering eyes, are gay.[11]

The final line has come back to me at the bedsides of hospice patients, ready for death and patient with its slow coming; and when I see grandparents and great-grandparents applauding the efforts of the very young, rejoicing in the hope they represent; and when I myself, as aging continues to happen, imagine my own final years. That line, among many others, has helped to equip me for those years in ways I keep discovering, as does another, which begins a blessing we hear in our congregation every Sunday at the completion of the Eucharistic celebration: "Life is short, and we do not have too much time to gladden the hearts of those who travel the way with us. So be swift to love and make haste to be kind. . . ."[12] Gaiety and gladness deserve a bit more mention in the catalogue of virtues we hope to help one another cultivate. Naming them is a beginning.

I'd like to end this chapter by commending to you the work of three contemporary wordsmiths whose gift for life-affirming laughter is worth enjoying and emulating. However humor is given to us, they show us, it is a service to the community to welcome it and make way for it on the page or over meals or in meetings or in the singular moments of encounter each day affords. It is leaven that helps our daily bread to rise and expand.

## Brian Doyle

A devoted husband and father and devout Catholic, deeply engaged in ecumenical conversation, Brian Doyle, who died too young a few years ago, begins one of his many short essays, "My son Liam was born ten years ago. He looked like a cucumber on steroids. He was fat and bald and round as a cucumber on steroids."[13] His irreverence is rooted, paradoxically, in the freedom afforded by deep faith and a foundational reverence for and delight in life in all its forms. He writes, for instance, in a short essay about raptors, "I have been so hawk-addled and owl-absorbed and falcon-haunted and eagle-maniacal since I was a little kid that it was a huge shock to me to discover that there were people who did not think that seeing a sparrow hawk helicoptering over an empty lot and then dropping like an anvil and o my god coming up with wriggling lunch was the coolest thing ever."[14] In an interview, he described himself as "swimming and thrashing and singing in [words] ever since I was two and three and learning to make sounds that turned people around in the kitchen and made them laugh or occasioned sandwiches and kisses or sent me to my room, ever since I was four and five and learning to pick out letters and gather them together in gaggles and march them in parades and enjoy them spilling down pages and into my fervent dreams."[15]

If there is, and I absolutely believe there is, such a thing as "holy laughter," Doyle's work invites us to it. His poems, essays, and talks consistently remind us and invite us to be at play in the fields of the Lord. Because of all people, those who live in "sure and certain hope" and who know themselves to be loved can afford to laugh.

### Anne Lamott

Anne Lamott's wild popularity over the past couple of decades suggests how widespread is the need for candor about spiritual confusion, political outrage, angst about single parenting, and regret over bad decisions about alcohol and drugs—as well as the widespread need for good writing, good speaking, lively connection, and laughter. Among many memorable words of encouragement to aspiring writers, she reminds them and us,

> When writers make us shake our heads with the exactness of their prose and their truths, and even make us laugh about ourselves or life, our buoyancy is restored. We are given a shot at dancing with, or at least clapping along with, the absurdity of life, instead of being squashed by it over and over again. It's like singing on a boat during a terrible storm at sea. You can't stop the raging storm, but singing can change the hearts and spirits of the people who are together on that ship.[16]

As with the craft of writing, Lamott makes faith more accessible, imaginable, and appealing while remaining focused on the growing clarity of her own faith journey (about which she has been very public) with fierce fidelity. On forgiveness, for instance, she writes simply, "Not forgiving is like drinking rat poison and then waiting for the rat to die."[17] And on hope: "Hope is not about proving anything. It's about choosing to believe this one thing, that love is bigger than any grim, bleak shit anyone can throw at us."[18] Laughter, she believes, is "carbonated holiness."[19]

One wonders, reading Lamott, whether the living water
Jesus promised might have a little fizz to it.


**David James Duncan**

The too-oft-quoted comment attributed to Voltaire that
"God is a comedian playing to an audience that is too
afraid to laugh" seems a bit reductive, but it's worth pausing over long enough to recognize that fear of laughter can
and does affect a certain bandwidth of pious people. Duncan, like Lamott and Doyle, addresses that fear head-on,
especially in his rich collection of essays, *God Laughs and
Plays: Churchless Sermons in Response to the Preachments of
the Fundamentalist Right.* He offers in the same collection
a wild inventory of those who offer perspectives on God
and truth that need to be kept in the ongoing conversation
among all of us who seek God and Truth:

> Contemporary politicized fundamentalists, includ-
> ing first and foremost those aimed at Empire and
> Armageddon, need us nonfundamentalists, mystics,
> ecosystem activists, unprogrammable artists, agnos-
> tic humanitarians, incorrigible writers, truth-telling
> musicians, incorruptible scientists, organic garden-
> ers, slow food farmers, gay restaurateurs, wilderness
> visionaries, pagan preachers of sustainability, com-
> passion-driven entrepreneurs, heartbroken Muslims,
> grief-stricken children, loving believers, loving dis-

believers, peace-marching millions, and the One who loves us all in such a huge way that it is not going too far to say *they need us for their salvation.*[20]

They—we—at least need all those folks to nudge us into awareness of a world with possibilities "broader than the measures of the mind" and a God who can live with our laughter.[21]

# Quit Trying to "Win"

Here are some alternatives to "winning": inviting, exploring, musing, modeling, reframing, reflecting, challenging. Draft a constitution for South Africa that allows old antagonists a way out of social gridlock and tribal peoples a way to maintain their traditions. Write a manifesto for a nonprofit dedicated to mitigating climate change that defines the common good with patient particularity. Report what one city accomplished by collecting food scraps for community composting. Write children's stories that enable little readers to locate themselves in a world where watersheds and bioregions matter more than state lines and relationship to other species is not only imaginative but realistically imaginable.

The way to civil conversation that loosens political and theological gridlock lies through a gray area, through a thicket of ambiguities and intersecting striations of problems, over tectonic plates riddled with the fault lines of ancient enmities. We navigate the minefield of public conversation, laced with trigger words and loaded images, using the light we're given. If we venture out there at all, into the public forum, we may have to do so like Frodo, accepting the call, but admitting that we do not know the way. For Frodo, taking the fatal ring was an act of love and trust in those, like Gandalf and Aragorn, whose wisdom he relied on. Our efforts to speak for and with others, making our own journeys through dark thickets of threat and deception and past fiery places where battles become violent, are at their best similarly acts of trust, driven by a love that will not let us be silent.

We will, at some point, be called upon to speak up and speak out, either by election to office or appointment to a committee or invitation to a podium, or by parenting elementary-school children who are encountering forms of hatred and harm from which they deserve protection. When that time comes, we need, as we face audiences that are divided, hurting, and defensive, to be "wise as serpents, and harmless as doves" (Matt. 10:16 KJV). We need to speak courageously, but also strategically, generously imagining those whose views oppose our own—what concerns them, what frightens them, what may have led them to the positions they take. Brian McClaren has pointed out that people across the political spectrum appear to share a number of core values, such as fairness, loyalty, and love of family, but in different order of priority. Imagining those with whom we differ in these terms—as people whose values may overlap with ours more than we know—it may be easier to broach our differences as something to explore rather than as the stakes in a battle to be won or lost.

Argument comes easily to us in this culture—some might say naturally. We all remember childhood disputes that consist mostly of "You did, too!" "I did not!" and, perhaps later, more dignified efforts to prove our points in classrooms or on debating teams where one stood to "win" a good grade or a round in a tournament. Some of us have spent years of Sundays attending churches where sermons often took the form of arguments against atheism or agnosticism or secular skepticism and for the authority of Scripture. The better ones, as I recall, didn't. The best revisited parables and invited us to reflect on the richness and surprise of love represented in biblical stories—even the puzzling ones. Theological and political arguments have their place, but they may do less to persuade the unpersuaded than their participants think. It may be that persuasion, in fact, isn't the point. Most of us don't live by propositions so much as by attractions, affections, affinities. We align ourselves with those whose lives touch ours in ways that awaken us, who address our hopes or needs, whose words stay with us because something in them rings true and opens our hearts as well as our minds.

We are, I think, most often persuaded by story, which is why so much of the world's wisdom literature takes that form. Good teaching tales don't corner you into agreeing but invite you into a new landscape where you can see things from a vantage point you might never have achieved without them. They work by paradox and surprise rather than by rational argument or presentation of empirical evidence.

Most of us learned in English classes to line up our points and make a "strong argument" for a point of view. An argument, teachers carefully explain—as I have from the front of many classrooms—isn't just a list of reasons lined up on the "pro" or "con" side of a proposition, but a line of reasoning that works from both principles and examples, pays attention to defining key terms, and makes appropriate concessions, because no human perspective offers the "whole truth." I would also add that the best arguments begin with story or incident. Something happened to make me understand, believe, and embrace a point of view I now want to share. What exactly happened—therein always lies a tale. If we begin with that tale, we take our hearers or readers with us on a journey that may leave them, and perhaps us, in a new place.

A professor who did more than any other to change my approach to writing and speaking sat me down with a paper I'd written and said, "Your writing is very architectural. You build a case, brick by brick, and it's a good, solid case, but you leave nothing for the reader to discover or wonder about. Don't think of yourself as building an edifice, but as conducting a tour of territory you'd like your reader to see and appreciate. Show them things along the way. Turn some corners and let them be taken by surprise." Shifting those metaphors helped me shift my focus from arguing a case to sharing some insights.

When you don't feel the need to win, you're free to play. You're free to pause and ponder and meander a little and reflect and invite and engage. My favorite writers do this. Annie Dillard has been a beloved model for years. Her wide, deep curiosities are contagious, as are her capacity for "beginner's mind" and her pleasure in surprise, which seems to greet her everywhere she looks because the world is, in fact, unlikely and irregular and sometimes shocking in itself. She doesn't have to convince her readers to care for the earth because her own caring is so electric and alive with fascination. Her articulate invitations to look closely at the life of a spider or the flight pattern of a mockingbird or the branchings of a tree, and her wild descriptions, change how we see them. They will never look the same again.

Urgencies are all around us. We do, if we care about disputed public issues, want to change people's minds and hearts. I want people to care about the health of the soil and the life of bees. I want Americans to care about the consequences of oil drilling and fracking and what plastics are doing to the ocean. I want parents to care about what's happening in underfunded schools. I want us together to imagine how our justice system might work more justly and how we might stop mass incarceration. I'm aware that even to name those issues is to use words that trigger conditioned responses—sometimes knee-jerk reactions. I am tempted to argue about them, especially with people who seem glib or willfully ignorant. I recognize that temptation as one to avoid where possible, not out of fear, but in hope of finding a way into conversation that offers inviting alternatives to confrontation.

## CHAPTER 12

Quakers are good at this. In what they call "threshing sessions," Friends gather to pray over, reflect on, and hear one another on difficult issues that have arisen in their communities. As one document explains, a threshing session is

> a meeting at which a variety of different, and sometimes controversial, opinions can be openly, and sometimes forcefully, expressed, often in order to smooth the passage of business at a later meeting for business (see Britain Yearly Meeting's Quaker Faith & Practice, §12.26). A threshing meeting can be arranged in order to share factual information, air one's views about a controversial subject, express our preferences, or ask questions. . . .
>
> No decisions are made at threshing meetings. The aim is simply to move towards clarity and a greater understanding of an issue and to separate the "grain of truth from the chaff." . . . A threshing meeting or session is usually moderated or facilitated by an experienced Friend, who is asked in advance to take on this role. The facilitator/moderator is responsible for making sure that everyone present has a chance to speak and air their views. Care should be taken to ensure that Friends of differing opinions can and do attend the threshing meeting or session. Friends with specific knowledge about the subject under discussion should be asked to present factual or complex material and be available to answer questions. Some-

one should also be asked to take notes at the meeting
for future reference.[1]

Their foundational commitment to peaceful process
has motivated Quakers throughout their history to develop
approaches to difficult questions, to threats to the community, and to political violence in the broader community
that provide alternatives to argument that escalates into
battle. I know from experience—both my own for a time
and that of lifelong Quakers (or Friends, as they call themselves, who are also my friends)—that all their meetings for
deliberation begin with clear, stated intention, silence, and
a time for each person present to speak his or her concern
without challenge or cross-talk. A brief silence follows each
contribution. Only after everyone who wishes to speak has
spoken is there discussion. Since the aim is unanimity, dis-
cerning the right course together, there are no votes. If they
hit a roadblock in their efforts to find agreement, they return to silence in which all seek further clarity until they
can converge on a resolution. It's a slow process. Efficiency
isn't the point; nor is winning.

Deliberate slowing down is countercultural. It challenges all the metaphors about racing—to the top, for the
cure, keeping our eyes on the prize, even the frequently
quoted passage in Hebrews that describes the life of a fol-
lower of Jesus as running "the race that is set before us"
(Heb. 12:1). It challenges us to be still and listen for guidance and wisdom and clarity. The current online popularity

of a Thai proverb attests to a widespread longing for that stillness: "Life is so short, we must move very slowly." Mindfulness is incompatible with the hurry that characterizes so many days for so many of us. As hurrying becomes a habit, we may not take stock of the losses we suffer in consequence, and slowing down becomes harder.

When I manage to slow down, though, I am aware of something coming back to me—energy, clarity, a sense of the center, a sense of connection to the world and to God. People express this experience in various kinds of language, but the discoveries seem to be universal. When we slow down, we wake up. We hear and see differently. We walk our paths with more surety and intention. We become less anxious. We listen. We "walk in beauty," as Lord Byron puts it; or, as Paul charges the Ephesians to do, we "walk in love" (Eph. 5:2 RSV).

Three writers who have modeled for me what that free-spirited, inquisitive, resilient, compassionate reflection looks like are these.

### Immaculée Ilibagiza

In the midst of one of the most horrific massacres in modern times, Ilibagiza, huddled in a hidden bathroom with three other women, hiding from Hutu killers on a rampage, prayed without ceasing. When she emerged, a survivor, she sought no revenge. Instead, she sought out some of the killers to extend forgiveness. She tells her story in *Left to Tell: Discov-*

*ering God amidst the Rwandan Holocaust.*[2] Reminiscent of the remarkable stories of forgiveness and reconciliation that emerged from South Africa in 1996, her story shows a way to live beyond violence and bigotry with an open heart, a sense of divine presence, and no fear of death. Her purpose is not to win political battles but to help others awaken, as she was awakened, to the fact that love is a force greater than death and unlike any other power on earth.

## Adania Shibli

In short vignettes in her short book *Touch* (seventy-two pages), the writer presents, in spare, prose-poetic style, what a young Palestinian girl sees as she moves about her home and village.[3] Too young to put deprivation, violence, death, and domestic tension in their larger context, she registers what is happening without moral judgment. Observations and feelings are threaded into a slow, sobering, ultimately heartbreaking narrative that allows the reader to imagine the suffering of a Palestinian child from inside out. In its way, this novella, without explicit political statement, makes as powerful a case as any made from a flag-draped podium for recognizing and stopping the decimation of Palestinian homes, families, and lives. "Her signature style," critic José García wrote in 2017, "comes from holding back."[4] Fiction gives her a forum, and with it she appeals to the imagination rather than to ideas, and to human sympathies that still cross political boundaries when innocents are harmed.

## Arundhati Roy

One of the most articulate, aware, courageous political activists in contemporary India, Roy has written and spoken around the world against abuse of economic power by multinational corporations and the "American Empire." Her essays show what deft, informed argument looks like. These are collected in books with names like *The Cost of Living, War Talk, Public Power in the Age of Empire, Broken Republic, Capitalism: A Ghost Story*, and *Things That Can and Cannot Be Said*. She is no stranger to controversy, and I am thankful every time I read her for her political vision, as incisive as it is broad.

In the United States she is perhaps best known, though, for her fiction. Her first novel, *The God of Small Things*, like Shibli's *Touch*, invites readers to imagine and reflect on the effects of national and international forces on a young girl as they disturb the life of a single family. Rahel, the central character and narrator who first appears at the age of seven, observes, "at times like these, only the Small Things are ever said. The Big Things lurk unsaid inside."[5] Roy's fiction offers its own way into reflection and action, educating her readers in a way that has inspired many to protest in the original sense of the word—to step up and speak for, on behalf of, the suffering—in a way that challenges abuse of power even as it awakens us to what it might mean to choose life in the very face of death.

# Afterword

The final lines of one of Edna St. Vincent Millay's sonnets, which I came to love as a romantic adolescent, have stayed with me as a valuable standard against which to measure my motives when I write and teach, hoping to keep my work relational, and to do it with a servant's heart:

> Love in the open hand, no thing but that,
> ungemmed, unhidden, wishing not to hurt,
> as one would give you cowslips in a hat
> swung from the hand, or apples in her skirt,
> I bring you, calling out, as children do,
> "Look what I have!—And these are all for you."[1]

Writing is finally a love relationship with the Spirit who meets us in our seeking and our imagining. "Offering" is a valuable verb. Our writing, our public speaking, our conversation is our offering to God, to the world, to those who matter to us, and to those who perhaps don't matter as much as they should. We bring what we have and what we can, given our time, energy, competing commitments, particular gifts, histories, limitations, and passions, trying to be obedient to our calling. The call comes through circumstances—accidents, losses, conversations, encounters on the street, dreams, news stories, insults, and other people's insights shared in writings that link us in a network more vast than we can map. We don't have to map it. We just have to stand where we are and where we must and speak about what's given with specificity, humility, boldness, awakened imaginations, gratitude, and grace, and with the clarity to which, as creatures who do not live by bread alone, but also by words, we are called.

# Questions for Discussion

## Introduction

- Consider your life with words. What's your "listening diet" in the course of a day? When are you most voluble? When do you tend to remain silent or retreat into silence?
- When and where have you witnessed good examples of what it means to "speak peace"?
- What words do you cherish and return to with gratitude?

## Chapter 1: Don't Rely on Webster's

- Consider how you have come to understand a particular word and how you might define it for a young person—"mercy" or "maturity" or "leadership" or "trust," for instance. What matters to you most that people understand about the term you chose?
- When have you heard or read a word history that has

enriched your understanding of the word? How has an antique usage—of "charity" in the King James Bible, for instance—enlarged or changed your understanding of what the word includes?

- What is an example of a word whose common meaning has shifted or changed significantly in the course of your lifetime? How might that have happened?

- When have you been inclined to resist new ways people are using a word or expression—"awesome," for instance, or "friend" or "care"?

- When have you found a speaker's use of abstractions evasive or inadequate or annoying? What example might you give? What specifics might have helped foster clarity and understanding?

- If you were to write a whole reflection or op-ed piece about a single term, what term might it be?


## Chapter 2: Unmask Euphemisms

- When have you noticed a matter of consequence being disguised or distorted by euphemistic descriptions of the kind discussed at the beginning of this chapter? Consider, for example, language used to refer to old age, obesity, pain, or greed.

- When, in recent reporting on matters of public concern, have you felt more careful distinctions need to be made?

- What euphemisms do you recognize that you habitually use? What purposes might they be serving?
- The term "campaign" has a military history dating back to the practice of leaving the fortress to take to, and take over, an "open field" (Latin: *campania*). How does knowing that word history affect the way you think about various appropriations of the term, like, for instance, an institution's "capital campaign"?
- What do you consider two or three of the most dangerous or problematic euphemisms in common public use now?

**Chapter 3: Remind People of What They Know**

- What do you find you need to be reminded of by family members, spiritual leaders, news reporters, poets, or storytellers?
- What books, documents, or sacred texts do you feel you benefit by rereading? In what ways has rereading or reviewing familiar material been surprising or helpful?
- How might you, personally, understand the challenge put to college students in one school's motto: "Remember who you are and what you represent"?
- What purposes has repetition served in your daily life?
- What is an example of a way that remembering the past has clarified for you what is needful in the present?

## Chapter 4: Embrace Your Allusive Impulses

- What famous phrases or sentences come back to you as useful and convenient reference points?
- How have you noticed that allusions to the Bible or Shakespeare or current films work in conversations with friends either to solidify connection or, less positively, to reinforce a kind of clubbiness?
- What is an example of an allusion that has added power and depth to someone's point?
- How can allusions connect us with the past and provide an important reminder of the historical dimension of our own thoughts or experiences?
- Consider what resonances, memories, and associations come up around a single word like "mountaintop" or "fiery" or "leap."

## Chapter 5: Tell It "Slant"

- When has an article or speaker or poet helped you see something familiar from a new angle? Do you remember particular "ways of putting it" that made you see differently?
- How do you understand the difference between "slant" and "bias"?
- When has it made a difference in your understanding and attitude to see something from much closer

or much further away? How has language helped you change your distance on what you think you know?
- What might happen if you told an incident from your own life in the third person ("she" or "he") rather than first person ("I")?
- What experience has taught you to reframe?

## Chapter 6: Promote Poetry

- Why do we need poets and poetry?
- When has a poem been of particular—even life-changing—importance for you?
- How do you understand the value of learning poetry or passages from carefully crafted texts by heart? When have you done that, and what difference has it made?
- What kinds of boundaries do poets often cross or question? How?
- In what places and ways might you begin to share more poetry?

## Chapter 7: Articulate Your Outrage

- "Righteous anger" is a term to use carefully and selectively. When is it warranted?
- When have you witnessed, or practiced, undue or even dangerous docility?
- What contributes to right recognition of the right moment for public expression of outrage?

QUESTIONS FOR DISCUSSION

- How do both the articulation of and the responses to public anger tend to be gendered?
- When have you paid a price for anger that you felt, and feel, was necessary? What makes it worth the cost?

## Chapter 8: Find Facts and Check Them

- What complicates fact-gathering and fact-checking?
- How do you determine which news sources to trust?
- How can commitment to factual accuracy contribute to peacemaking?
- Consider what kinds of facts it might take adequately to describe to a young person the processes involved in climate change?
- How are facts and myth or story of complementary importance?

## Chapter 9: Mind Your Metaphors

- What's an example of a dangerous or misleading metaphor?
- What's an example of an illuminating or helpful metaphor?
- What metaphors are commonplace in your family culture?
- How far can you develop the rich anatomical metaphor of "a body" in describing either the church or the state?

- What are some examples of how metaphors related to electronics, computers, or other high-tech machines have provided ways to describe ourselves and our communities? With what effects?

## Chapter 10: Complicate Matters

- What is one example of what you regard as dangerous oversimplification?
- Give an example of what it might mean to simplify without dumbing down.
- When have you attempted to honor the complexity of a process or chain of causality even under pressure to speed up and simplify? What happened?
- When people come up with the common response to why they broke off a relationship with the words, "It's complicated," what kinds of complications might they be referring to?
- Consider what happens when you "widen the lens" on a problem you've tended to describe in a set of terms you've gotten used to—family conflicts, for instance, or a child's behavior problems, or stagnation in a working group?

## Chapter 11: Laugh When You Can

- I have come across the term "holy laughter" in spiritual writing. How might you understand it?

- When have you witnessed authentic, life-giving laughter that invites, encourages, and unifies?
- Why is it important to laugh at what is truly ridiculous? Give an example.
- What is one of your favorite examples of verbal humor—wording that surprises readers or hearers into laughter?
- In what circumstances do you feel it's important to remind ourselves that we can "afford" to laugh?

## Chapter 12: Quit Trying to "Win"

- In what ways have you found that contests can be counterproductive?
- Competitiveness is widely regarded as a virtue in our culture. When does it become destructive?
- How do you think you're most effectively persuaded of a point of view about which you have uncertainties?
- What happens when you open up an argument to three or more "sides" or points of view?
- How does debate tend to make discernment harder?

## Afterword

- How might you work specifically on making your words an offering? A form of service? A source of encouragement or surprise?

# *Notes*

**INTRODUCTION**

1. Richard J. Mouw, *Uncommon Decency: Christian Civility in an Uncivil World*, 2nd ed. (Downers Grove, IL: InterVarsity, 2010), 13–14, citing Martin Marty.

**CHAPTER 1**

1. Frederick Douglass, *Great Speeches by Frederick Douglass* (Mineola, NY: Dover, 2013), 35.

2. Elie Wiesel, "The Perils of Indifference," speech delivered before President Bill Clinton, April 12, 1999. http://www.history place.com/speeches/wiesel.htm.

3. T. S. Eliot, "Little Gidding," in *Four Quartets* (New York: Mariner Books, 1968), 55.

4. Wendell Berry, *The Memory of Old Jack* (Berkeley: Counterpoint, 1999), 112.

5. James F. Childress, "The War Metaphor in Public Policy: Some Moral Relections," in *The Leader's Imperative: Ethics, Integrity, and Responsibility*, ed. J. Carl Ficarrotta (West Lafayette, IN: Purdue University Press, 2001), 181–97.

6. *Speeches and Letters of Abraham Lincoln, 1832–1865* (New York: E. P. Dutton, 1907), 26.

7. Paraphrased by Ursula K. Le Guin, *The Language of the Night: Essays on Fantasy and Science Fiction* (New York: HarperCollins, 1992), 204.

**CHAPTER 2**

1. George Orwell, "Politics and the English Language," in *The Collected Essays, Journalism, and Letters of George Orwell*, vol. 4 (Boston: Nonpareil Books, 2000), 139.

2. Naomi Wolf, *The Beauty Myth* (New York: Harper Perennial, 2002), 257.

3. Stephen Miles, *Oath Betrayed: Torture, Medical Complicity, and the War on Terror* (New York: Random House, 2006), introduction.

4. "Making Murder Respectable," *The Economist*, Dec. 17, 2011, https://www.economist.com/international/2011/12/17/making-murder-respectable.

5. Jeremy Fyke and Kristin Lucas, "Euphemisms and Ethics: A Language-Centered Analysis of Penn State's Sexual Abuse Scandal," June 1, 2013, https://epublications.marquette.edu/cgi/viewcontent.cgi?article=1101&context=comm_fac.

6. Mariette Grange, "Smoke Screens: Is There a Correlation between Migration Euphemisms and the Language of Detention?," *Global Detention Project Working Paper Number 5*, Oct. 15, 2013, https://papers.ssrn.com/sol3/papers.cfm?abstract_id=2340390.

7. Lomi Kriel, "Longer Stays Leave Record Number of Immigrant Children in Detention," *Houston Chronicle*, Nov. 21, 2018.

8. Tanvi Misra, "Report Finds Harsh Conditions at Immigration Detention Centers," *The Atlantic*, Oct. 7, 2015, https://www.theatlantic.com/politics/archive/2015/10/report-finds-harsh-conditions-at-immigration-detention-centers/433035/.

9. Steven De Schrijver, "The Future Is Now: Legal Consequences of Electronic Personality for Autonomous Robots," *Who's*

*Who Legal*, https://whoswholegal.com/features/the-future-is -now-legal-consequences-of-electronic-personality-for-auton omous-robots.

10. BBC News, Oct. 19, 2006, posted at https://electronicinti fada.net/content/bbc-publishes-list-key-terms-used-israel-pal estinian-conflict/6463.

11. Shoshana Zuboff, *The Age of Surveillance Capitalism: The Fight for a Human Future at the New Frontier of Power* (New York: PublicAffairs Books, 2019).

12. Sir William Harcourt, MP, "A Letter on the Perils of Inter-vention," in *Letters of Historicus on Some Questions of International Law* (London: Macmillan, 1863). Posted at https://sites.tufts.edu /reinventingpeace/2013/08/30/sir-william-harcourt-on-human itarian-intervention-150-years-ago/.

13. Richard Falk, "The Complexities of Humanitarian Inter-vention: A New World Order Challenge," *Michigan Journal of In-ternational Law* 17, no. 2 (1996): 491–513.

14. Tim Fernholz, "The World Bank Is Eliminating the Term 'Developing Country' from Its Data Vocabulary," May 17, 2016, https://qz.com/685626/the-world-bank-is-eliminating-the-term -developing-country-from-its-data-vocabulary/.

**CHAPTER 3**

1. Naomi Wolf, *The End of America: Letter of Warning to a Young Patriot* (White River Junction, VT: Chelsea Green Publishing, 2007), 27.

2. "I Love to Tell the Story" by Kate Hankey (1866), tune by William G. Fischer (1869), https://hymnary.org/text/i_love_to _tell_the_story_of_unseen_thing.

3. Wendell Berry, *The Country of Marriage* (Berkeley: Coun-terpoint, 2013), 14–15.

4. Wendell Berry, *The Art of the Commonplace* (Berkeley: Counterpoint, 2003), 58.

5. William Bryant Logan, *Dirt: The Ecstatic Skin of the Earth* (New York: Norton, 2007), 91.

6. William Bryant Logan, *Air: The Restless Shaper of the World* (New York: Norton, 2012), 32.

7. Arundhati Roy, *The Cost of Living* (New York: Modern Library, 1999), 105.

## CHAPTER 4

1. Chana Bloch, "Blood Honey," in *Blood Honey* (Pittsburgh: Autumn House Press, 2009), 60.

2. Lucille Clifton, "Sorrow Song," in *The Collected Poems of Lucille Clifton* (New York: BOA Editions, 2012), 263.

3. Walt Whitman, "As Adam in the Early Morning," in *Whitman: Poetry and Prose* (New York: Library of America, 1982), 267.

4. Walt Whitman, "To Workingmen," in *Whitman: Poetry and Prose*, 89.

## CHAPTER 5

1. T. S. Eliot, "East Coker," in *Four Quartets* (New York: Mariner Books, 1968), 16.

2. Lewis Hyde, *Trickster Makes This World: Mischief, Myth, and Art* (New York: Farrar, Straus and Giroux, 2010), 208.

3. David Quammen, *Natural Acts: A Sidelong View of Science and Nature* (New York: Norton, 2008).

4. Mary Oliver, "Wild Geese," in *New and Selected Poems*, vol. 1 (Boston: Beacon, 1992), 110.

5. Nadia Bolz-Weber, *Pastrix: The Cranky, Beautiful Faith of a Sinner and Saint* (New York: Jerico Books, 2013).

6. Jon Pareles, "An Appraisal: Leonard Cohen, Master of Meanings and Incantatory Verse," *New York Times,* Nov. 11, 2016.

7. From Cohen's "Anthem" on his 1992 album *The Future.*

**CHAPTER 6**

1. Kim Rosen, *Saved by a Poem: The Transformative Power of Words* (Carlsbad, CA: Hay House, 2009).

2. Etheridge Knight, "Hardrock Returns from the Hospital for the Criminal Insane," in *The Essential Etheridge Knight* (Pittsburgh: University of Pittsburgh Press, 1986), 7.

3. Annie Finch, "Poetry Diplomacy in the Congo," Poetry Foundation Blog, Apr. 13, 2012, https://www.poetryfoundation .org/harriet/2012/04/poetry-diplomacy-in-the-congo.

4. From Mary Oliver, "Lead," in *New and Selected Poems*, vol. 2 (Boston: Beacon, 2005), 54.

5. Susan Spady, "Two," in *Claiming the Spirit Within*, ed. Marilyn Sewell (Boston: Beacon, 1996), 209.

6. Annie Stenzel, "An Incantation for the Small Hours of the Night," *Academic Medicine* 82, no. 3 (March 2007): 290.

7. Rafeef Ziadah, "We Teach Life, Sir," on spoken-word CD (Hadeel, 2009). Available at https://store.cdbaby.com/cd/rafeef ziadah2.

8. Ellen Bass, "Dead Butterfly," in *The Human Line* (Port Townsend, WA: Copper Canyon, 2007), 45.

9. Naomi Shihab Nye, "Different Ways to Pray," in *Words under the Words: Selected Poems* (Portland, OR: Far Corner Books, 1995).

10. Li-Young Lee, "Praise Them," http://www.poetry-chaikhana .com/blog/2010-12-10/li-young-lee-praise-them/.

11. Chana Bloch, "Blood Honey," in *Blood Honey* (Pittsburgh: Autumn House, 2009), 59.

12. Debra Spencer, "At the Arraignment," featured on https:// writersalmanac.publicradio.org/index.php%3Fdate=2005%252 F03%252F13.html, March 13, 2005.

## CHAPTER 7

1. Chris Hedges, "The Coming Collapse," *Truthdig*, May 20, 2018, https://www.truthdig.com/articles/the-coming-collapse/.

2. Cornel West, *Race Matters* (Boston: Beacon, 2001), 85.

3. Michelle Alexander, *The New Jim Crow: Mass Incarceration in the Age of Colorblindness* (New York: The New Press, 2012), 164.

4. Timothy Snyder, *On Tyranny: Twenty Lessons from the Twentieth Century* (New York: Tim Duggan Books, 2017).

5. W. H. Auden, *Collected Poems* (New York: Vintage, 1991), 141.

6. Max Wynn, "Marian Wright Edelman Delivers Stirring Speech," Dec. 6, 2013, https://luskin.ucla.edu/marian-wright-edelman-delivers-stirring-speech/.

7. Dietrich Bonhoeffer, *No Rusty Swords*, ed. Edwin Robertson (New York: Harper & Row, 1970), 221.

8. Quotes are taken from "The Power of Martin Luther King's Anger," aired on *All Things Considered*, NPR, Feb. 20, 2019.

9. Sherman Alexie, "Sherman Alexie," *The Progressive*, Jan. 29, 2012, https://progressive.org/dispatches/sherman-alexie/.

## CHAPTER 8

1. Harvey Wasserman in podcast, "Fukushima—a Global Threat That Requires a Global Response," popularresistance.org, Oct. 12, 2013.

2. Joshua Cohen, "Troublesome News: Numbers of Uninsured on the Rise," *Forbes*, July 6, 2018, https://www.forbes.com/sites/joshuacohen/2018/07/06/troublesome-news-numbers-of-uninsured-on-the-rise/#3ac469fb4309.

## CHAPTER 9

1. Ephrat Livny, "The Sum of Your Parts: The Simple Metaphor

That's Increasingly Getting in the Way of Scientific Progress," *Quartz*, Sept. 9, 2017, https://qz.com/1072039/the-simple-metaphor -thats-increasingly-getting-in-the-way-of-scientific-progress/.

2. Stephen Ginn, "Metaphors in Medicine," *BMJ*, Aug. 23, 2011, https://blogs.bmj.com/bmj/2011/08/23/stephen-ginn-meta phors-in-medicine/.

3. J. Vyjeyanthi S. Periyakoil, MD, "Using Metaphors in Medicine," *Journal of Palliative Medicine* 11, no. 6 (2008): 842–43.

4. Paul Willis, unpublished open letter to the faculty of Westmont College.

5. George Barna, *Marketing the Church: What They Never Taught You about Church Growth* (Colorado Springs: Navpress, 1988), 13–15.

6. Tim Schraeder, "4 Must-Know Church Marketing Secrets," *Church Leaders*, May 9, 2019, https://churchleaders.com/worship /worship-articles/160080-4-must-know-church-marketing-se crets.html.

7. Information from the North American Bear Center, https:// bear.org/what-if-i-get-between-a-black-bear-mother-and-her -cubs/.

**CHAPTER 10**

1. Karen Fiser, "Still Life with Open Window," in *Losing and Finding* (Denton: University of North Texas Press, 2004), 36.

2. John Keats, letter to George and Tom Keats, Dec. 27, 1817, in *The Letters of John Keats, 1814–1821*, vol. 1, ed. Hyder Edward Rollins (Cambridge, MA: Harvard University Press, 1958), 193.

3. Megan Gannon, "Race Is a Social Construct, Scientists Argue," *Scientific American*, Feb. 5, 2016, https://www.scientificamer ican.com/article/race-is-a-social-construct-scientists-argue/.

4. Esteban Ortiz-Ospina and Diana Beltekian, "How Is Literacy Measured?," *Our World in Data*, June 8, 2018, https://our worldindata.org/how-is-literacy-measured.

5. T. S. Eliot, "The Wasteland," in *The Wasteland and Other Poems* (Toronto: Broadview, 2011), 64.

**CHAPTER 11**

1. Brian Doyle, *Book of Uncommon Prayer* (Notre Dame, IN: Sorin Books, 2014), 41.

2. From the hymn "There's a Wideness in God's Mercy" by Frederick William Faber (1862).

3. T. S. Eliot, "The Dry Salvages," in *Four Quartets* (New York: Harcourt, 1971), 39.

4. Richard Wilbur, "The Eye," in *New and Collected Poems* (San Diego: Harvest Books, 1988), 57.

5. Avner Ziv, "Humor as a Social Corrective," in *Writing and Reading across the Curriculum*, ed. Laurence Behrens and Leonard J. Rosen, 3rd ed. (Glenview, IL: Scott, Foresman, 1988), 356–60.

6. G. K. Chesterton, "Authority and the Adventurer," in *Orthodoxy* (New York: John Lane, 1908), 298–99.

7. U. A. Fanthorpe, "Getting It Across," in *Selected Poems, 1978–2003* (Upton Cross, Liskeard, Cornwall: Peterloo Poets, 2005).

8. See Michael Tlanusta Garrett et al., "Laughing It Up: Native American Humor as Spiritual Tradition," *Journal of Multicultural Counseling and Development* 33 (Oct. 2005): 194–205.

9. See Eric Schwitzgebel, "The Humor of Zhuangzi: The Self-Seriousness of Laozi," in *The Splintered Mind*, Blogspot, Apr. 8, 2013, http://schwitzsplinters.blogspot.com/2013/04/the-humor-of-zhuangzi-self-seriousness.html.

10. See Koenraad Elst, "Humour in Hinduism," in *Humour in Religion*, ed. Hans Geybels and Walter van Herck (London: Continuum, 2011), 35–53.

11. William Butler Yeats, "Lapis Lazuli," in *The Collected Poems of W. B. Yeats: A New Edition*, ed. Richard Finneran (New York: Macmillan, 1989), 294.

12. Paraphrased from Henri Frédéric Amiel, *Amiel's Journal* (Amazon Digital, 2012), 306.

13. Brian Doyle, "How We Wrestle Is Who We Are," in *The Wet Engine: Exploring the Mad Wild Miracle of the Heart* (Brewster, MA: Paraclete, 2005), 151.

14. Brian Doyle, "Raptorous," in *Children and Other Wild Animals* (Corvallis: Oregon State University Press, 2014), 55–57.

15. Brian Doyle, "The Way We Do Not Say What We Mean When We Say What We Say," in *Eight Whopping Lies and Other Stories of Bruised Grace* (Cincinnati: Franciscan Media, 2017).

16. Anne Lamott, *Bird by Bird: Some Instructions on Writing and Life* (New York: Anchor, 1995), 237.

17. Anne Lamott, *Traveling Mercies: Some Thoughts on Faith* (New York: Pantheon Books, 1999), 134.

18. Anne Lamott, *Plan B: Further Thoughts on Faith* (New York: Riverhead Books, 2005), 275.

19. Lamott, *Plan B*, 66.

20. David James Duncan, *God Laughs and Plays: Churchless Sermons in Response to the Preachments of the Fundamentalist Right* (Great Barrington, MA: Triad Books, 2006), 54–55.

21. The quote is from the hymn "There's a Wideness in God's Mercy" by Frederick William Faber (1862).

**CHAPTER 12**

1. Sue Glover Frykman, compiler, "Threshing Meetings/Sessions." Document used in the EMES Meeting for Learning, June 11–13, 2010, at Svartbäcken, Rimbo, Sweden. Found at https://www.fgcquaker.org/cloud/madison-friends-meeting/resources/what-threshing-session.

2. Immaculée Ilibagiza with Steve Erwin, *Left to Tell: Discovering God amidst the Rwandan Holocaust*, rev. ed. (Carlsbad, CA: Hay House, 2014).

3. Adania Shibli, *Touch*, trans. Paula Haydar (Northampton, MA: Clockroot Books, 2010).

4. José García, "Adania Shibli on Writing Palestine from the Inside," *Literary Hub*, Feb. 6, 2017, https://lithub.com /adania-shibli-on-writing-palestine-from-the-inside/.

5. Arundhati Roy, *The God of Small Things* (New York: Random House, 1997), 136.

**AFTERWORD**

1. Edna St. Vincent Millay, "Not in a Silver Casket Cool with Pearls," in *Collected Sonnets of Edna St. Vincent Millay* (New York: Harper, 1941), 80. Also accessible at https://www.americanpoems .com/poets/ednamillay/not-in-a-silver-casket-cool-with-pearls/.

# Bibliography

Many, but not all, of the works listed below are mentioned in this volume. Not all represent points of view I agree with. Some not mentioned in these chapters have been included here because of their relevance to parts of this conversation—and because I can't imagine thinking about current public discourse without them. I have listed poets separately, including suggested poems or collections, hoping they will provide an incentive to explore these poets further. Similarly, the short list of websites and online resources is a tiny selection of a rich range of material out there that I hope readers will explore to follow any threads and curiosities this book left dangling for further exploration.

## Books Worth Reading and Rereading

Alexie, Sherman. *Ten Little Indians*. New York: Grove, 2004.
Barna, George. *Church Marketing: Breaking Ground for the Harvest*. Colorado Springs: Regal Books, 1992.

Begbie, Jeremy. *Resonant Witness: Conversations between Music and Theology*. Grand Rapids: Eerdmans, 2011.

Berry, Wendell. *Hannah Coulter*. Berkeley: Shoemaker and Hoard, 2005.

———. *Standing by Words*. Berkeley: Counterpoint, 2011.

Bolz-Weber, Nadia. *Salvation on the Small Screen?* New York: Seabury, 2008.

Bonhoeffer, Dietrich. *The Collected Sermons of Dietrich Bonhoeffer*. Minneapolis: Fortress, 2012.

Chesterton, G. K. *Orthodoxy*. Louisville: GLH Publishing, 2016.

Childress, James, Alan Melnick, and Richard Bonnie. *Essentials of Public Health Ethics*. Burlington, MA: Jones and Bartlett Learning, 2013.

Douglass, Frederick. *Great Speeches by Frederick Douglass*. Mineola, NY: Dover, 2013.

Doyle, Brian. *A Book of Uncommon Prayer*. Notre Dame, IN: Ave Maria Press, 2014.

Doyle, Brian, with David James Duncan. *One Long River of Song: Notes on Wonder for the Spiritual and Nonspiritual Alike*. Boston: Little, Brown, 2019.

Edelman, Marian Wright. *The Measure of Our Success: A Letter to My Children and Yours*. New York: Harper Perennial, 1993.

Ehrenreich, Barbara. *Bright-Sided: How Positive Thinking Is Undermining America*. London: Picador, 2010.

Fisk, Robert. *The Age of the Warrior: Selected Essays by Robert Fisk*. New York: Nation Books, 2008.

## Bibliography

Goodman, Amy, et al. *The Silenced Majority: Stories of Uprisings, Occupations, Resistance, and Hope*. Chicago: Haymarket Books, 2012.

Hedges, Chris. *War Is a Force That Gives Us Meaning*. New York: Public Affairs, 2014.

Ilibagiza, Immaculée, with Steve Irwin. *Left to Tell: Discovering God amidst the Rwandan Holocaust*. Revised ed. Carlsbad, CA: Hay House, 2014.

King, Martin Luther. *A Testament of Hope: Essential Writings and Speeches*. San Francisco: HarperOne, 2003.

Klein, Naomi. *This Changes Everything*. New York: Simon and Schuster, 2015.

Lamott, Anne. *Bird by Bird: Some Instructions on Writing and Life*. New York: Anchor, 1995.

Lewis, C. S. *The Four Loves*. San Francisco: HarperOne, 2017.

Logan, William Bryant. *Dirt: The Ecstatic Skin of the Earth*. New York: Norton, 2007.

McEntyre, Marilyn. *Caring for Words in a Culture of Lies*. Grand Rapids: Eerdmans, 2009.

McKibben, Bill. *Eaarth: Making a Life on a Tough New Planet*. New York: St. Martin's Griffin, 2011.

McLaren, Brian. *Naked Spirituality: A Life with God in 12 Simple Words*. San Francisco: HarperOne, 2012.

Miles, Stephen, MD. *Oath Betrayed: Torture, Medical Complicity, and the War on Terror*. New York: Random House, 2006.

Morrison, Toni. *The Source of Self-Regard: Selected Essays, Speeches, and Meditations*. New York: Knopf, 2019.

# BIBLIOGRAPHY

Mouw, Richard. *Uncommon Decency: Christian Civility in an Uncivil World.* Downers Grove, IL: IVP Books, 2010.

Orwell, George. *The Collected Essays, Journalism, and Letters of George Orwell.* Boston: David R. Godine, 2019.

Pappé, Ilan. *The Biggest Prison on Earth: A History of the Occupied Territories.* London: Oneworld Publications, 2017.

Payer, Lynn. *Medicine and Culture.* New York: Holt, 1996.

Pound, Ezra. *Literary Essays of Ezra Pound.* New York: New Directions, 1968.

Quammen, David. *Natural Acts.* New York: Norton, 2008.

Reich, Howard. *The Art of Inventing Hope: Intimate Conversations with Elie Wiesel.* Chicago: Chicago Review Press, 2019.

Rosen, Kim. *Saved by a Poem: The Transformative Power of Words.* Carlsbad, CA: Hay House, 2009.

Roy, Arundhati. *My Seditious Heart: Collected Nonfiction.* Chicago: Haymarket Books, 2019.

Scahill, Jeremy. *Dirty Wars.* New York: Bold Type Books, 2013.

Shibli, Adania. *Touch.* Northampton, MA: Clockroot Books, 2010.

Snyder, Timothy. *On Tyranny: Twenty Lessons from the Twentieth Century.* New York: Tim Duggan Books, 2017.

Stevenson, Brian. *Just Mercy: A Story of Justice and Redemption.* New York: Spiegel and Grau, 2014.

Storm, Hyemeyohsts. *Seven Arrows.* New York: Ballantine Books, 1972.

Taylor, Jeremy. *Dreamwork.* Mahwah, NJ: Paulist Press, 1983.

Tolkien, J. R. R. *The Tolkien Reader*. New York: Del Rey Books, 1986.

Wasserman, Harvey. *The Healing Road*. Indianapolis: Dog Ear Publishing, 2012.

Whitmire, Catherine. *Practicing Peace: A Devotional Walk through the Quaker Tradition*. Notre Dame, IN: Sorin Books, 2007.

Wills, Garry. *Inventing America*. New York: Vintage, 2017.

Wolf, Naomi. *The Beauty Myth: How Images of Beauty Are Used against Women*. New York: HarperCollins, 2009.

———. *The End of America: Letter of Warning to a Young Patriot*. White River Junction, VT: Chelsea Green Publishing, 2007.

## Relevant Websites

factcheck.org
mediabiasfactcheck.com
pdfs.semanticscholar.org
politifact.com
snopes.com
spj.org/ethicscode.asp
sunlightfoundation.com

## Poets and Poetry Worth Exploring

Auden, W. H. *Collected Poems*. New York: Vintage, 1991. (Also see his essays.)

Bass, Ellen, *The Human Line*. Port Townsend, WA: Copper Canyon, 2007.

Bloch, Chana. *Blood Honey*. Pittsburgh: Autumn House, 2009.

Cairns, Scott. *Slow Pilgrim: The Collected Poems*. Brewster, MA: Paraclete, 2015.

Carver, Raymond. *All of Us: The Collected Poems*. New York: Vintage, 1996.

Clifton, Lucille. *The Collected Poems, 1965–2010*. New York: BOA Editions, 2012.

Cohen, Leonard. *The Lyrics of Leonard Cohen*. London: Omnibus, 2009.

Eliot, T. S. *Collected Poems, 1909–1962*. London: Faber and Faber, 2002.

Fanthorpe, U. A. *New and Collected Poems*. London: Enitharmon, 2010.

Fiser, Karen. *Losing and Finding*. Denton: University of North Texas Press, 2004.

Knight, Etheridge. *The Essential Etheridge Knight*. Pittsburgh: University of Pittsburgh Press, 1986.

Lee, Li-Young. *The Undressing: Poems*. New York: Norton, 2018.

Nye, Naomi Shihab. *Words under the Words: Selected Poems*. Portland, OR: Far Corner Books, 1995.

Oliver, Mary. *New and Selected Poems*. 2 volumes. Boston: Beacon, 2007.

Qabbani, Nizar. *Arabian Love Poems*. Colorado Springs: Three Continents, 1999.

# Bibliography

Stenzel, Annie. *The First Home Air After Absence.* Boston: Big Table, 2017.

Willis, Paul J. *Rosing from the Dead.* Seattle: WordFarm, 2009.

Yeats, W. B. *The Collected Poems of W. B. Yeats.* New York: Macmillan, 1989.

Ziadah, Rafeef. *We Teach Life.* Video and CD release, Nov. 23, 2015.